FROM HOPE TO HIGHER GROUND

ALSO BY MIKE HUCKABEE:

Quit Digging Your Grave with a Knife and Fork

Available from Center Street

FROM HOPE TO HIGHER GROUND

My Vision for Restoring America's Greatness

MIKE HUCKABEE

GOVERNOR OF ARKANSAS

CENTER STREET

New York Boston Nashville

Center Street
Hachette Book Group USA
237 Park Avenue
New York, NY 10017
Visit our Web site at www.centerstreet.com.

Printed in the United States of America

Originally published in hardcover by Hachette Book Group USA.

Center Street is a division of Hachette Book Group USA, Inc.
The Center Street name and logo is a trademark of Hachette Book Group USA, Inc.

First Trade Edition: February 2008
10 9 8 7 6 5 4 3 2 1

The Library of Congress has catalogued the hardcover edition as follows:
Huckabee, Mike.
   From hope to higher ground : 12 stops to restoring America's greatness / Mike
Huckabee.
       p. cm.
   "Governor Mike Huckabee of Arkansas presents a vision for what America can become
with the right kind of leadership, a clear direction, and a people who are willing to believe
that the World War II generation doesn't have to be the last 'greatest generation.'"
—Provided by the publisher.
   ISBN-13: 978-1-59995-704-3
   ISBN-10: 1-59995-704-3
   1. United States—Social conditions—21st century. 2. Conduct of life. 3. Life skills—
United States. I. Title.

HN59.2.H837 2007
646.700973—dc22   2006024374

ISBN 978-1-59995-155-3 (pbk.)

The people of Arkansas have afforded me their trust and their encouragement for the ten and a half years it was my pleasure to serve as their governor. They didn't ask for me when they first got me, but kept me when they had a choice. They repeatedly revealed the best spirit of greatness by showing their desire to serve and sacrifice. They gave me the best job in the world and I only hope that I gave them the best I had within me by the grace of God.

To the wonderful people of my home state and treasured home, Arkansas, I dedicate this book.

ACKNOWLEDGMENTS

I'm pretty sure this book would have been better had it been ghost-written by someone else, but I don't do well giving someone else's speeches or publishing a book I didn't actually write. The message in these pages is solely mine. It's not intended to be a textbook or an exhaustive work with minute details as to how I would personally save the world. I don't have that much confidence in myself and wouldn't advise you to either. My hope and optimism for America is not rooted in what I think or what I've done. There's a long line of people in public life who can tell you why they are smarter, more experienced, better prepared, and more illuminated than I can hope to be.

My hope comes first from God, who I believe has given this nation a great gift and with it a great responsibility, but it also comes from my belief that the true greatness of America is in its everyday people, who do great things without being elected to a position or given a title. They not only fight our wars and shed their blood, but they coach our kids in baseball and give hugs and bowls of soup to hungry strangers.

While the message of this book is mine, it was not a work done in a vacuum. It couldn't have happened without the encouragement of my literary agent, Margret McBride of the McBride Agency and Donna DeGutis, Faye Atchinson, and Ann Bomke. The publisher and editors at Hachette Book Group (formerly Time Warner) and their Center Street imprint division believed in me when I wrote *Quit Digging Your Grave with a Knife and Fork*, and were willing to take another chance with me and have the presses roll with this effort. Rolf Zettersten and his dedicated staff, especially Harry Helm, Lori Quinn, Christina Boys, Meredith Pharaoh, Dylan Hoke, and Jody Waldrup, have been patient, professional, and personable. I have been made to feel like a part of a real team and not just another author peddling his prose.

If it "takes a village" to raise a child, then it was almost a village that helped me prepare the manuscript for actual publication. There were dictation tapes to transcribe, rewrites for grammar and spelling and structure to check, and content reviewed for clarity. Thanks are due to Dawn Cook, Brenda Turner, and Kelly Boyd from my staff, who used some after-hours and weekends to look things over and make suggestions, and my daughter-in-law, Lauren, who transcribed most of the chapters in their original form while between semesters of law school, as well as my wife, Janet, and daughter, Sarah, who typed some of the handwritten corrections and helped me hit the deadline by assisting in the typing of the final version. My sons, John Mark and David, offered their critiques as well, making it a family project in many ways. I can't acknowledge the family without mentioning that I was never alone for a single word I wrote since my nearly nine-year-old Labrador retriever, Jet, was at my side along with his "little brother," the toy shih tzu named Sonic that provided companionship at all hours of the day and night, and comic relief when my brain stopped functioning.

Finally, thanks to every person who ever voted for me and who believed in me and hired me to do something that was more joy than job.

CONTENTS

CONTENTS

PART I

Hope Is Where It Starts

HOPE IS WHERE IT STARTS

For me, "hope" is more than a word that describes the American spirit. Every time I hear it I think of home. I was born August 24, 1955, in Hope, Arkansas, a tiny town of about eight thousand people. Except for its claim to fame as Home of the World's Largest Watermelon, Hope had pretty much escaped notice until it became known as the birthplace of Bill Clinton, forty-second president of the United States.

My ancestors settled in Hope in the early 1800s and every male in my lineage before me lived his entire life there. I, too, was raised and educated there, and was the first male in my family bloodline to graduate from high school. When I left Hope to go to college, I became the first male to leave except for the occasional short stint of those who served in the military or who worked in the shipyards temporarily during World War II.

In many ways I wish every American could have had a childhood like mine and could have been raised in Hope. It was a wonderful community. A child could leave his house in the morning on a bicycle and not return until after dark, and it caused no one alarm. It was the kind of place where I could misbehave eight blocks from home, but by the time I pedaled back to 509 East Second Street, six people would have called my parents to report my behavior. I am not sure that it took a village to raise a child, but I am quite sure that an entire village did its part to help raise me!

My job at the local radio station as a teenager led me to believe that I would have a career in some form of broadcasting or communications and eventually to become active in politics and run for public office. Because of my deep personal faith, it seemed logical to assume that my life would be immersed in applying those communication skills to an evangelical organization.

By the time I was twenty-one, I was the director of a full-service faith-based advertising agency in Texas and involved in producing television programs, publications, advertising, and public relations for one of the nation's fastest-growing evangelical organizations. I supervised a staff of twelve artists, writers, and production specialists and was responsible for a multimillion-dollar budget.

By the time I was twenty-five, I was ready to come back to Hope, Arkansas, to operate a communications business and start laying the groundwork to run for public office. I ghostwrote books; wrote, produced, and placed advertising; and designed publications for churches, Christian ministry and mission organizations, and even some commercial businesses. Things were falling into place for me to begin taking my first political steps when I encountered a detour that took me down a road I wasn't planning to travel.

A church in Pine Bluff, Arkansas, asked me to come and speak on a Sunday because they were without a pastor. Their pastor had recently resigned and they were looking for various people to fill in during their search for a new minister. Following that Sunday, they asked me if I could come to speak for a week-long series of services. They then asked me to serve as the interim pastor for a few months while they searched for a permanent replacement. Three months later, they asked to remove the "interim" label and I spent six of the most wonderful years of my life as pastor of the Immanuel Baptist Church of Pine Bluff. In addition to the church work, I led the launch of a twenty-four-hour-a-day local community television channel.

Involvement in the community was something I not only preached but practiced. I served as president of the local unit of the American Cancer Society, worked in United Way, served on the board for the local multi-church outreach to combat homelessness and poverty, and was active in the local Chamber of Commerce.

Somehow running for public office while simultaneously serving as a pastor seemed incompatible so I gave up that notion. After six years in Pine Bluff, the Beech Street First Baptist Church of Texarkana, Arkansas, invited me to lead that congregation, which I had the joy of doing for an additional six years. As in Pine Bluff, I also led in the creation of another community television channel for the Texarkana area, which broadcast everything from high school football games to talk shows to church services. In Texarkana, I again became active in the community, serving on numerous boards, including the Chamber of Commerce, United Way, and Friendship Center, an area philanthropic organization that assists the unemployed and families with food, rent, and clothing.

During this time, I was elected as the youngest ever president of the Arkansas Baptist State Convention, a denomination that represented one in every five Arkansans.

Running for office had ceased being an option for me during those years as a pastor, but friends from several directions began asking me if I'd ever thought of running for office, not knowing the long suppressed dreams from nearly a dozen years ago.

By now, my wife, Janet, and I had achieved a level of comfort neither of us had ever dreamed. We were both thirty-six years old, had three children, a good dog, and lived in a nice five-bedroom home with a pool on a cul-de-sac. We were involved in the community and had wonderful friends, a good salary, and a fine reputation. Why on earth would we leave such a pleasant and comfortable life to get involved in politics?

I vividly remember the long walk in the neighborhood we took one winter night. We decided that if we indeed were put on earth to become "comfortable," then we had hit the target. Ours was an enviable life in many ways, but as we walked and talked and prayed, we decided that the purpose for being on earth is not our personal comfort but to strive to make the world better for our children than when we found it.

Our journey had begun in Hope, but it was about to be anything *but* higher ground!

I resigned my position with the church and, in early 1992, announced my candidacy for the United States Senate. My opponent would be a former governor and three-term U.S. senator. Despite all odds, I was convinced I could and would win.

I didn't.

Instead of feeling the whole effort had been a mistake, Janet and I both felt that it was simply the beginning of a long and uncertain process. We had spent our entire savings down to our last dime to make the Senate race. I was without a job or a regular paycheck. We had started our marriage with nothing but enough used furniture to barely fill a two-room apartment we rented for a grand total of $40 a month, and here we were, eighteen years later, starting over.

With a mortgage, three school-age children, and nothing in savings left, my wife and I were truly tested. She went to work as a unit clerk in the ICU unit at St. Michael Hospital in Texarkana, working the 11 p.m. to 7 a.m. overnight shift. I restarted my communications business, consulting other communities on developing local television stations, and also picked up some writing and advertising projects. I even served as an interim pastor in a small church on weekends. In spite of overwhelming odds, we never missed a payment or were even late for our obligations, although to this day, I count it as nothing short of a miracle that we made it through those months.

I was asked by then state Republican Party chairman Asa Hutchinson to consider running for lieutenant governor in a special election in 1993. Bill Clinton's election as president placed Jim Guy Tucker in the governor's office and created a vacancy for lieutenant governor. The organization from my unsuccessful Senate campaign was still intact, and I agreed to do it, though at the time I wasn't sure why anyone, including me, would want to be lieutenant governor!

Building an army of grassroots volunteers, we overcame a huge money disadvantage and disproved political conventional wisdom by winning in the special election in July 1993.

My victory wasn't celebrated at the Democratic State Capitol (I was the *only* Republican constitutional officer and only the fourth elected statewide since Reconstruction). The doors to my office were spitefully nailed shut from the inside, office furniture and equipment was removed, and the budget essentially spent down to almost nothing prior to our arriving. After fifty-nine days of public outcry, the doors were finally opened for me to occupy the actual office I had been elected to hold two months earlier.

After being reelected in 1994 to a full four-year term as lieutenant governor by the highest margin of any Republican in the state's history, I became governor on July 15, 1996. My predecessor, Jim Guy Tucker, had been forced to resign due to felony convictions in federal court on issues related to a financial scandal he was involved in prior to being governor. For a while, partisan critics called me "the accidental governor" until I asked them whose accident had cause me to be governor? I never heard that again.

My becoming governor clearly incensed those on the left, who throughout my tenure loved to label me the "Rev-Gov" or the "Huckster," obviously thinking that attacking my background as a person of faith and a pastor would scare people. Those who wrote letters to the editor and sent them anonymously to me feared I would replace the Capitol Dome with a steeple and legislative hearings with Wednesday night prayer meetings!

Rather than feel my background was a detriment, I felt it was a tremendous asset. My experience dealing every day with real people who were genuinely affected by policies created by government gave me a deep understanding of the fragility of the human spirit and the vulnerability of so many families who struggled from week to week.

I was in ICU at 2:00 a.m. with families faced with the decision to disconnect a respirator on their loved one; I counseled fifteen-year-old pregnant girls who were afraid to tell their parents about their condition; I spent hours hearing the grief of women who had been physically and emotionally clobbered by an abusive husband; I saw the anguish in the faces of an elderly couple when their declining health forced them to sell their home, give up their independence, and move into a long-term-care facility; I listened to countless young couples pour out their souls as they struggled to get their marriages in survival mode when confronted with overextended debt, sudden and unexpected unemployment and loss of income, or the anxieties of having a child with severe disabilities.

My experiences helped me to better understand that good government is not about policies, but about the people whose lives are going to be touched.

From my teenage years working at the J. C. Penney store in Hope, where I cleaned windows and floors and stocked shelves, I learned that hard work tends to give one a softer heart for others. To this day, I am careful not to touch the glass on the door when I enter a store, knowing someone will have to wipe the fingerprints and smudges later. I can remember my frustration when immediately after scrubbing a glass door, I would watch helplessly as someone with grimy hands bypassed the door handle and pushed on the glass, voiding my work and prompting a call from the manager to clean the doors.

For many Americans, life is hard. Certainly even Americans at the edge of poverty still live better than most of the world's population, but that doesn't mean life for them is easy or without risk and struggle. Most mothers and fathers have great hopes for their children to live a better life than they themselves have lived. Parents often make great sacrifices and work extra jobs to provide opportunities for their children because they truly hope that their efforts will boost the chances and choices for their kids and their descendants. As long as that hope exists, parents will work an extra job, take a sandwich in a paper sack instead of eating out at lunch, and forgo new clothes or cars to save for their child's opportunities.

Should circumstances become so overwhelming that the parent feels he or she is "below sea level" with the floodwaters rising, that parent is in danger of giving up hope, and when that happens, the sacrifices stop and the excuses and desperation take over. When hope is lost, all is lost, and generations can be subject to settling for mediocre existence.

Below Sea Level

In the final days of August 2005, Hurricane Katrina, a category five storm, ravaged the Gulf Coast of the United States, striking hardest against the shores of southern Mississippi and at the heart of one of America's truly unique cities, New Orleans, Louisiana. The impact of the hurricane itself was devastating enough, shattering windows, ripping roofs from homes and commercial buildings, and sending hundreds of thousands of Gulf Coast residents fleeing for their lives out of the path of one of the most ferocious hurricanes to be charted by the National Weather Service. In a matter of hours the "Big Easy" became the "Big Mess." For New Orleans, however, the worst was yet to come.

New Orleans is not only unique for its culture of spicy food, authentic Dixieland jazz music, all-night bars, and nonstop entertainment. It is set apart by the fact that it was established as a city below sea level, protected by a series of levees that surround the Crescent City. Engineers and hydrologists had predicted devastating floodwaters should anything ever breach those levees.

While America watched, courtesy of twenty-four-hour news channels eager to bring the most sensational and epic pictures to viewers, the levees did in fact seep and then pour water. Within hours the once bustling streets of New Orleans turned into raging rivers that forced those citizens left behind into a desperate search for a spot of dry ground. Tens of thousands sought what was thought to be temporary shelter in the Louisiana Superdome, home to some of the great sports and entertainment spectacles of the past generation from Super Bowls to mega-concerts, as well as of the nation's largest conventions.

Not too far away, the New Orleans Convention Center also became a refuge as the ravaging waters continued to rise. Thousands upon thousands of others were unable to make it to the designated shelter areas and were forced to cling to chimneys and vent pipes on rooftops or to try to find safety camped out on the bridges of Interstate 10.

For the next several days, Americans watched in horror, then disgust, and ultimately in anger as they saw their fellow citizens stranded and, for all practical purposes, abandoned without food, shelter, or even water, and with very little hope of response from any level of government. Over the coming months much debate would center on why the response to this tragedy seemed so inept. A long line of critics waited their turn to point fingers at local, state, or federal officials. Armchair analysts offered confident and conclusive summations on what had gone wrong, who was at fault, and what should be done to prevent such a disaster in the future.

I had been with the Southern Governors' Association at Mercer Plantation in Georgia when I received news of the impending hurricane. After ten years as governor I knew a hurricane on the Gulf Coast (or even the threat of one) meant thousands of anxious people would be fleeing their homes in Mississippi, Louisiana, or Texas, and heading as far north as necessary to find shelter, food, and a place to get away from the assault of the hurricane. I cut my trip short, arriving home in Little Rock just before the Hurricane hit the coast, to begin preparing our state for what would certainly be an extraordinary influx of evacuees escaping the coastal areas to get to higher, and hopefully dryer, ground. Being an inland state, Arkansas doesn't experience hurricanes, so when they threaten to strike our nation's coastline we don't brace for property damage but we do brace for "people damage." Those who cross into our borders often come filled with the trauma of having barely gotten ahead of the storm, or at the very least filled with anxiety as to what will await them upon their return.

As we coordinated with our usual partners for these type events, such as the Red Cross, and began stocking up facilities and supplies, I was kept abreast of the situation like other Americans by watching the news reports on television. I literally wept as I saw the desperate faces of children, elderly people, and frantic parents waving at rescue boats or passing helicopters. The rescue vessels were pushed way past capacity as brave first responders sought to pluck victims from danger, and stage rescues in the flooded waters of neighborhoods. Some people held on to nothing more than parts of ice chests, which served as their makeshift flotation devices and life-saving instruments.

"Dear God," I prayed, "this is not Rwanda or Kosovo or a Third World fishing village in Asia! This is the United States of America—the most powerful and the wealthiest nation on earth—and here are thousands upon thousands of fellow Americans. We can get a television camera to them, but we seem to be incapable of getting a lifeboat or even a bottle of water to them!"

I was ashamed of what appeared to be an uncontrolled natural disaster met with an incomparable incompetence to respond to it. Within a day or two local shelters that had been prepared in civic centers and church gymnasiums were reaching capacity, and it became apparent that the numbers fleeing north toward our state for safety would eclipse anything we had experienced before.

I called an emergency cabinet meeting of the heads of all the major state agencies. I asked each one to compile a list of available resources that could be used not only in the rescue and recovery efforts along the coast but also to assist in the temporary relocation of thousands of storm victims who would be crossing our borders. A command center was hastily set up in the Governor's Conference Room on the second floor of the State Capitol. Within two hours this massive room, normally used for larger meetings and press conferences, became home to more than thirty state employees who worked around the clock at folding tables, surrounded by computer screens, television sets, and banks of phones.

Members of my staff worked alongside agency heads and employees from various state departments enlisted for levels of expertise ranging from phone skills to proficiency in logistics, transportation, and communicable disease. They would answer what we anticipated to be an overwhelming volume of phone calls both from evacuees needing assistance as well as citizens calling to volunteer and offer a helping hand. A call center was also established in a state-owned building just across the street from the Capitol. Within four hours of the order to create it, fifty volunteers manned fifty telephones while stationed at computer terminals, all assembled in an amazing flash of time by technical experts from our state's Department of Information Systems and the office of our chief information officer.

As we began to get reports of hotel space being filled at the northern borders of Arkansas, federal officials informed us that we would likely be receiving several thousand additional evacuees by airlift, and we had to prepare for many more people than originally planned.

From my years in church and faith-based work I realized there were dozens of church- and denominational-owned camps throughout the state that had closed their camping season within the previous few weeks. That meant they were empty but not yet shut down for the winter.

I summoned Chris Pyle, a valued team member and policy advisor for family and faith-based issues, to my office. Chris had been with me since the day of my swearing in some ten years earlier. I tasked him to get on the phone and contact the major denominational offices and churches that we knew operated summer camps. In addition we called upon Boy Scout, Girl Scout, and 4-H camps, which would also likely be available. We asked the leaders of these denominations, churches, and civic organizations to come to the Governor's Mansion the following day for an emergency meeting to discuss coordinating the relief efforts.

Mass disasters and evacuations often lead to a compounded problem where the already overwhelming trauma is exacerbated by the dehumanizing experience of losing a sense of personal identity with people being forced to move en masse as part of a throng of humanity. It had troubled me greatly as I watched so many thousands of evacuees from the Gulf Coast being moved into mass shelters and stacked like human boxes on top of one another with little regard for their privacy or their personhood.

At the meeting with denominational and nonprofit leaders who owned camps I was humbled by the 100 percent participation and agreement to reopen the camps throughout the state to help house evacuees. Chris Pyle, along with volunteers from our office, surveyed each of the camps to determine how many beds and what kind of dining and recreational facilities and configurations of sleeping quarters would be available in each of the camps.

I had told our cabinet the day before and now reiterated to these partners from the faith and nonprofit sector that the mission would be "to take care of people first and fill out the paperwork later."

While we were certainly concerned about the cost of what would inevitably be massive expenses for housing, feeding, clothing, and assisting these evacuees, our first mission was to simply follow the Golden Rule: "Do unto others as you would have them do unto you."

I challenged everyone working in our relief efforts to ask this simple question, "How would I want to be treated if it were me?" Each person was told that if they saw a seven-year-old coming off a bus or airplane, "Treat them how you would want your own seven-year-old to be treated in such a circumstance." When seeing an elderly and bewildered person, ask, "If this were my grandmother, how would I want someone to treat her?" Once we established the Golden Rule criteria for all our operations, everything else got much easier.

Officials from the Federal Emergency Management Agency (FEMA) had told us on the Friday before Labor Day that we would be receiving approximately four thousand evacuees, arriving via airlift at the Fort Smith, Arkansas, airport. We would initially take them to Fort Chaffee, a military post operated by the National Guard for processing, and then transport them to one of the many camps that were hastily reopened for one of their most unusual and challenging housing experiences ever.

In a matter of twenty-four hours, camps that had been recently closed came alive again as cooks were enlisted, maintenance personnel were brought back to make sure that showers and utilities were operational, and food was purchased. Volunteers prepared to feed those who would be coming with literally nothing but the clothes they had on their backs.

Based on instructions from FEMA officials, National Guard troops stationed at Fort Chaffee prepared what was to be an initial breakfast meal for the four thousand we were anticipating to arrive at 7:00 a.m.

Seven a.m. came and went and no one had arrived. Eight, nine, and ten o'clock came and still no sign of evacuees or any airplanes. Repeated calls to federal officials produced conflicting answers, none of which turned out to be accurate or consistent with the messages before or after. By late afternoon we instructed officials at Fort Chaffee as well as at the various faith camps to stand down their operations and wait for further notice. Hopefully more reliable information as to who would be coming, how many, and where would be coming soon.

Throughout the afternoon and evening, reports continued to surface of groups of evacuees, ranging from dozens to hundreds, scheduled to arrive on planes or buses at any moment.

None came.

Then, shortly after midnight on that Saturday night, and for the next five hours, approximately ten thousand people began raining on Fort Chaffee much like the waters of the hurricane had rained upon New Orleans just days before. Meanwhile, planeload after planeload descended upon the Fort Smith airport, exceeding available ground transportation to get them from the airport to Fort Chaffee, and obliterating plans for an organized entry for these people.

Repeated calls to FEMA were fruitless, so I placed a desperate call to contacts at the White House and pleaded for their intervention in getting flights diverted from Fort Smith, which was being overwhelmed. We begged them to go to Little Rock, where we were prepared to triage the needs and process the next wave of evacuees. Several terse conversations and even a couple of shouting matches with federal officials finally resulted in planes landing at Little Rock. We had assembled buses and volunteers from local church and medical teams to help care for those who just hours before had lived in the squalor of the Superdome or Convention Center, or perhaps hung to life on overpasses or rooftops. They had been hastily boarded onto a variety of conveyances from military aircraft to commercial charters to buses.

Because of the amazing resilience and resourcefulness of a large number of heroic state employees and volunteers, we were able to process the thousands of evacuees and get them food, bedding, fresh clothing, and perhaps as important, a smile and a much needed hug of human compassion.

In the course of less than a week, an estimated 75,000 people poured into Arkansas seeking refuge from the storm and relief from the trauma. That number increased our state's population by 3 percent in a five-day period. And while many of the news organizations camped out at the Houston Astrodome praised the efforts of Texas to house more than 200,000 evacuees, Texas would have had to absorb nearly 800,000 evacuees to feel the impact at the same proportion as Arkansas. That is in no way to take anything away from the noble, unselfish, and sacrificial efforts of our neighbors and friends from the great state of Texas. It merely puts in perspective the scope of the effort made by the Arkansas people I've loved, served, and have never been more proud of.

Our strategy for disseminating the masses of people throughout the entire state meant that no one single geographic area would have its infrastructure of health care, education, or employment overwhelmed by an influx number of evacuees. The impact would be distributed evenly across the state. Rather than bringing them all to a single facility such as the ALLTEL Arena in North Little Rock, we divided evacuees into groups of a few hundred people in a church or scout camp to ensure that if a communicable disease or an outburst of violence occurred, it could be contained and would affect only a few hundred rather than tens of thousands.

We had committed to each of the camps that we would provide what we termed a "mayor" and a "police chief." We enlisted retired state troopers, retired mayors, and others who had experience in administration of civil government and law enforcement to provide twenty-four-hour-a-day supervision and security. This was not because we feared what the evacuees might do, as they generally turned out to be gracious, peace-loving, and grateful models of citizenship. We needed to protect them from exploitation. We wanted to give them something that they had not experienced in several days and that was a feeling of welcome and security.

It was our mission and commitment to provide more than sand-wiches, cots, showers, and clothes, but most of all to provide a human touch, and to enlist enough volunteers so that every person who found himself or herself a temporary involuntary resident of our state would experience being called by name and treated with dignity and respect. It was and remains my firm conviction that regardless of a person's color, gender, or economic station in life, every person deserves to be treated in such a way.

The outpouring from the churches and faith-based groups was beyond anything we could have imagined. In fact, we simply had not fully antici-pated the level of compassion that people *would* give. We had expected to need more state-provided staffing for the camps and had underestimated that the church groups who operated the camps would have at their dis-posal thousands of ready, anxious, willing, and well-equipped volunteers who canceled their Labor Day weekend plans and took leave from work in order to come and make beds, stir soup, organize recreational activi-ties, sort and organize clothing, and provide loving human care to their neighbors and fellow citizens.

During the Katrina ordeal, most Americans saw our nation at one of its lowest moments with governments at all levels incapable of meeting what turned out to be an overwhelming wallop of a natural storm, com-bined with a lack of a plan for evacuation and rescue. But while it was a demonstration of America at its worst, it was also a demonstration of America at its best.

As government failed, its people did not.

As officials in charge often fretted over paperwork and proper forms to be filled out, ordinary citizens became extraordinary heroes simply by helping people and giving them hope.

In the weeks and months following Katrina's devastating impact on our coastline, congressional hearings, news conferences, and endless inches of newspaper space were filled with second-guessing and blaming. As I sat and listened to the individuals rescued from New Orleans tell their personal stories, I was mindful that cameras could not record the greatest tragedy of Hurricane Katrina and later Hurricane Rita.

It was not the shattered buildings of glass, wood, and steel, or the flattened and flooded homes that brought stark reminders of the capacity of a killer storm. It was not even the images of National Guard troops patrolling American streets darkened without utilities, emptied except for an occasional looter. The real images were beyond the camera lenses, very deep inside the souls and hearts of the human beings whose lives had been shattered far worse than any window and whose frames of confidence had been bent worse than any steel girder.

As we saw victims of Hurricane Katrina overwhelmed by the unexpected storms and surges of water that washed away their hope, we also saw ourselves as likewise being vulnerable. We are reminded that in many ways we *all* live below sea level, surrounded by levees that we think will hold and that we trust to keep us safe. But whether the levees are those made by human hands with concrete and steel, or are the levees of our personal health, our jobs, the safety of our neighbors, our pension plan, or the confidence we have placed in our government, churches, banks, or other institutions, all of us indeed live below sea level and are but one breached levee away from devastation.

Sadly, for too many Americans, the levees have been breached, the water is pouring in, and they are rapidly losing real hope. When hope is lost, all is lost. The will to seek higher ground is rooted in hope that the present calamity is not a permanent condition.

America today is a deeply troubled nation. But its primary problem is not a political but a perspective problem. There are deep divisions in our nation as people feel an alienation between Democrat and Republican, urban and rural, heartland and coast. Some observers have simplified it, describing the division of red states and blue states. Today, much of the public discourse is well beyond spirited debate or even disagreement. It's become true division as differences become lines of demarcation and even friends and family are separated from congenial fellowship because of a contentious factionalism.

The best moments that America has had were the moments in which

Americans sacrificed their self-interest for the greater good of others. Our worst moments are when our self-absorption leads to a "me first" mind-set, robbing us of the *"You-Nited States of America"*—to what has become the *"ME-Nited States of America."*

In my previous book, *Quit Digging Your Grave with a Knife and Fork*, I shared my personal pilgrimage of losing more than a hundred pounds and going from a classic "sofa spud" to a person who now runs two marathons a year and has given up traditional Southern fried foods and processed sugar. In that book, I candidly discussed my personal health journey and my secrets of succeeding at healthy living. I asserted then and now that the key to good behavior and a positive lifestyle is in identifying, confronting, and stopping bad behaviors and practices that are barriers to implementing good health habits.

In Part II of this book I've outlined twelve STOPs—not steps, but *STOPs* that need to be made before new and better choices and habits can be developed. Just as I needed to change my personal habits to regain my own health—so America must change its habits in order to regain its true greatness.

For this to happen, it's not just a matter of *steps* we must take but rather STOPs we must make. In this book I will outline what those *STOPs* are and how they can help us build bridges instead of barriers and help restore the American spirit of hope. At the end of each chapter, there will be a list of action *steps* as a way to prime the pump for personal or civic action.

Several years ago, I was part of an organization to help develop grassroots campaigns and encourage activists to get involved in their communities, states, and nation. It was called ACTION America and it stood for Activating Citizens To Impact Our Nation. I hope, as you complete each chapter, you will take steps to impact your world, and go from hope to higher ground.

PART II

12 STOPs to Restoring America's Greatness

Chapter 1

STOP BEING CYNICAL

Cynicism is the worst enemy of optimism. It is worse than negativism. The negative person often yearns to believe something will be better, but is fearful that believing is a setup for disappointment. The cynic, however, is not a mere doubter but actually scoffs at virtue, honor, duty, and humility, believing they are signs of weakness or, worse, are mere facades of duplicity and insincerity.

The worst reporters with whom I've dealt are not obnoxious because they are skeptics but because they are cynics. Skepticism is an admirable quality in a journalist and a desirable trait for one who wishes to practice good reporting marked by balance and objectivity. The cynic, however, goes beyond merely asking questions and seeking facts, and begins from the premise that authority figures—whether they be politicians, corporate CEOs, religious leaders, or sports or entertainment celebrities—have ulterior motives for everything they say and do. In the eyes of the cynic the public official who visits a school and chats with children is merely looking for a photo op. The entertainer who speaks out against social injustice is simply attempting to garner publicity for her new film. And the religious leader who builds an orphanage is attempting to build an empire.

Americans respond best to a message that is optimistic and hopeful. Most of us will cross the finish line of life far better than we anticipated when we left the starting block. Our American experiences give us every reason to believe that things can and will get better.

When I was eight years old the Bois d'Arc Lake was constructed by the Arkansas Game and Fish Commission near my hometown of Hope. It was a truly big event. This several-hundred-acre man-made lake would allow ordinary families to fish or hunt, and it was anticipated that in addition to wonderful recreational opportunities, it would also provide for flood control. The event was significant enough that it was to draw the attendance of then governor of Arkansas, Orval E. Faubus.

I still vividly remember my father saying, "Son, we're going to go to the lake dedication because the governor is coming to give the dedication speech and you may live your whole life and never get a chance to meet the governor in person."

I remember going to the dedication of that lake and seeing and shaking hands with the governor and indeed thinking that it was a once-in-a-lifetime moment for a kid like me to meet the governor.

Just over thirty-two years later I would be sworn in as Arkansas's forty-fourth elected governor. Unfortunately my father died of cancer three and a half months before the swearing in, and was not present to see that special day, but I've always felt that somehow he did get to see it from the grandstand of heaven.

My father was a fireman, and that job didn't pay enough for us to live on. On his days off he operated a small repair shop, where he worked as a mechanic rebuilding generators for cars. We rented the little house on East Second Street that we lived in until my parents were finally able to buy that house when I was in high school.

I'm a person of optimism because I know what it is like to go from a small rental house to living in the Governor's Mansion. I wasn't born with a silver spoon, but the streets were paved with golden opportunities afforded me by the schools I was able to attend, the teachers who encouraged me, and the parents who made great sacrifices so that I could obtain levels of education that were well beyond their reach. I wasn't endowed with a trust fund, but had a healthy trust that God would create opportunities. It would be my responsibility to accept those challenges and do well.

Having an optimistic spirit does not mean that life is filled with one great success after another. True optimism is the result of learning to overcome hardship and obstacles rather than living life without them. The most optimistic people I've encountered are the ones who have known hardship and trial, and the most cynical people are those who have yet to experience the kind of crisis that puts life in perspective and gives one a benchmark against which life's experiences are best evaluated.

"Attitude determines altitude" is a saying I've heard and repeated many times. A person who thinks he will succeed has a much greater likelihood of doing so than the person who is convinced that he will fail, for such a person is almost guaranteed to be correct. Attitude not only directs individuals but a nation as well. And when America is given optimistic and hopeful leadership, it responds accordingly. Whether one agreed with Franklin Delano Roosevelt's policies or not, his optimism in the face of his own personal struggles with polio was remarkable. His mantra that "the only thing we have to fear is fear itself!" provided the kind of leadership that helped America work its way out of the Great Depression and become a military superpower that eventually defeated enemies in both Europe and Asia in the Second World War. President Dwight D. Eisenhower presided over an unprecedented era of prosperity and educational advancement during the period of our nation's history when there was a great deal of optimism about the future. President John F. Kennedy charmed Americans with his winsome humor, but also challenged America with his vision to put a man on the moon within the decade. While an assassin's bullet kept him from seeing it come to pass, this nation did in fact conclude the decade by watching Neil Armstrong place his foot on the surface of the moon with the declaration that it was "one small step for man; one giant leap for mankind."

More recently, President Ronald Reagan endeared himself to Americans for his cheerful spirit and ability to crack a joke even while being prepped for surgery minutes after being wounded by a would-be assassin. His campaign in 1984, built around the theme of "Morning in America," led to a landslide reelection—quite a contrast to John Kerry's "misery index" in the 2004 presidential election. Voters want to elect someone who leads as if he is going somewhere wonderful, rather than the candidate who gives the impression that he is sorry for where he has been!

But it isn't only presidents who set the example of the positive effects of positive thinking. You've no doubt encountered people in your own life who have this spirit, as I did when I visited Dr. Robert Schuller, the founding pastor of the Garden Grove Community Church, in the spring of 2006. I had been an admirer of his for thirty years because of the life-lifting message that he called "possibility thinking," a unique blend of positive thinking and traditional faith that had brought hope and encouragement to so many people.

Dr. Schuller and his wife started their church with just the two of them arriving in California with a small organ in the back of a utility trailer and started holding church services in a drive-in movie theater. From those humble beginnings came the church known today to millions across the world as the Crystal Cathedral. It is one of the architectural wonders of the modern world, breathtaking in its beauty, creative in its design and its ingenious functional versatility. Large panels of crystal-like glass open along the entire height of the building to allow the fresh California air into the auditorium, giving it the capacity to be both an indoor and outdoor venue.

Far greater than the physical grandeur of the church, however, is the impact that Dr. Schuller has had during six decades of innovative and cutting-edge ministry. If there was any doubt of the authenticity of this man and his ministry, it was erased when I met his family. It was then I realized his most significant achievement was not a stunning architectural masterpiece, but a family who embodied the optimism, the kindness, and the openness of his messages. Dr. Schuller is not an optimist because of the absence of challenges in his life but because he has faced them and been able to work through them and beyond them.

My own optimism, both personally and for our nation, is not the result of having spent time on a mountaintop but from having spent so much time in the valley. The air tends to be thin on the mountaintop, but in the valley the soil is rich and good things grow there. It is in the depths of the valley that we discover our weakness but also our capacity for strength and resilience. Growing up in a family of modest means was not a curse but a blessing that gave me an appreciation for the things I have now and an extraordinary sense of gratitude for a life that has come a long way from used cars, a house without air-conditioning, and two-day vacations to visit relatives that never went beyond a neighboring state.

As an elementary school kid, I would start each school year with two pairs of blue jeans. The knees had holes worn through them by spring, and were patched with iron-on patches. At the end of the school year the legs were cut off to become shorts for the summer. Now when I put on a nice suit and tie I can't help but think, "It's quite a contrast from my early days!"

I started working at the age of fourteen at the local radio station in Hope, KXAR, and at a J. C. Penney in the stockroom. I worked throughout high school and paid my way through college and graduate school. I worked forty hours a week at a college town radio station, and carried enough class hours to complete my four-year degree in two years and three months, graduating magna cum laude. I didn't do that because I was that much smarter than my classmates, but because I was pretty sure I couldn't afford the cost of staying four years. I figured out that it was logistically possible to complete the hours necessary for my degree in just over two years if I would take the maximum number of classes allowed, test out of classes in which I was proficient, and go to sessions in the summers between regular semesters. I was barely twenty when I finished college.

I learned early in life that complaining, whining, or blaming others for my problems not only failed to garner much sympathy from those around me, but did nothing to improve my situation. While I never have nor will welcome unexpected upheavals in my comfort, I have learned that experiencing the harsh reality of our human frailty not only deepens us in strength and resolve but steeps us in a greater awareness of God's grace and presence, and removes from us the bitterness of cynicism.

Janet and I married on May 25, 1974, just a little more than a week after completing our first year of college at Ouachita Baptist University in Arkadelphia, Arkansas. We were both just a few months shy of our nineteenth birthdays. As I look back, I'm sure our families and friends thought we were out of our minds to get married at such a young age.

A few months after we married, Janet had taken leave from school to help me finish my degree. She worked as a dental assistant while I worked at the radio station and served as pastor of a small church and attended classes. In February 1975 she started experiencing back pain. When it did not get better, she went to a local doctor who diagnosed it as back strain from standing over dental patients all day, and prescribed medication and bed rest. Bed rest meant time off from work and loss of what little income she had, which was vital to our survival. After a week off work she returned, but there was continued and growing pain in her lower back.

Two doctors later she was recommended for several days of hospitalization and ultimately it was determined that she needed to see an orthopedic specialist in Little Rock, about an hour drive from Arkadelphia. The orthopedic surgeon examined her and confidently declared it was a "textbook case of a ruptured disc" and needed to be surgically repaired.

By now we had been married just over a year. In the fall of 1975, I was in my final semester of college and we were facing my twenty-year-old wife having surgery. In addition to her having to take off from work and lose income, the medical bills were staggering for a young couple in college whose income totaled $75 a week.

Arrangements were made for the surgery in Little Rock in mid-September 1975. The day before it was to be performed the doctor ordered a myelogram, a medical procedure in which dye is injected into the spinal column to determine the exact location of the disc that had ruptured and the extent of the damage.

I knew something was wrong when I was ushered into a small consultation room off the hallway of the hospital and asked to wait. The doctor came in with a face as white as his lab coat, and asked me to take a seat, and then proceeded to tell me that he wouldn't be doing the surgery the next day because the myelogram revealed that she didn't have a slipped disc after all. She had a tumor growing inside the canal of her spine. He said he would need to call in a neurosurgeon, who would talk with us and give us our options.

Dr. Thomas Fletcher was called in. This turned out to be providential. Not only was he one of the state's premier neurosurgeons, but a gentle and kind man. He walked into Janet's hospital room and could tell he was looking at two very scared kids who had thought all of life was in front of them, only to discover the very real threat that most of life might already be behind them. He explained that the tumor was a rare form of malignancy and because of its location inside the spinal canal, it was pressing against her spinal cord. There was a likelihood that the tumor would be inoperable, and in that case the cancer would be terminal. He hoped to get into the spinal canal and remove the tumor, but he prepared us for the likelihood that the operation could result in severing the spinal cord, leaving her paralyzed from the waist down for the rest of her life.

He gently told us that we could hope for something better but needed to be prepared for the worst. We will never forget his patience and his compassion as he broke the news to us and scheduled the surgery for a few days later.

On September 29, 1975, the day of the surgery, he had prepared us for what could be several hours in the operating room. After about two hours I looked up and was shocked to see Dr. Fletcher coming down the hall. He had already changed from his surgical scrubs into street clothes. I started to panic, thinking, "This can't be good if he is already finished."

He came in, smiled, and said that when he reached the tumor he was able to extract it and did not think there was permanent damage to the spinal cord but we wouldn't know for a few hours. One of the most precious sights in my life was seeing Janet's right and then left foot move after the anesthesia wore off, which was an affirmation that she would likely recover all functions.

To prevent the tumor from coming back it was recommended that she undergo radiation therapy. For the next six weeks, we got up at five each morning, and I loaded her into a makeshift bed in the back of our car. We drove the seventy miles to Little Rock for a 7:30 a.m. treatment of radiation therapy, then turned around and drove back to Arkadelphia, where I would attend class and then come home and take care of her in the hospital bed we had set up in our small two-room apartment. We paid all of $40 a month for that apartment! Between taking care of her and going to class, I still had to attend to my duties as pastor of a small church, which was now our only source of income.

Little by little, she learned to walk again and regained her strength, but the doctors had warned us that due to the intensity of the radiation therapy and the location of the tumor it would be unlikely that we would be able to have children due to probable damage to her ovaries.

The week before Easter 1976, I came home at lunch from class at graduate school and she told me that she was pregnant. It was one of the greatest joys of my life! We had "walked through the valley of the shadow of death." Now we were on the mountaintop.

November 28, 1976, our older son, John Mark, was born. He was more than our first child and a great gift from God, but a true miracle. Although we lost a child in pregnancy after John Mark, God did bless us with David, born July 22, 1980, and our daughter, Sarah, born August 13, 1982. Our greatest joy comes from the fact that we remain a close-knit family with three children who share our faith and even our strongly held political views.

There were times when I wondered why such a challenge would happen to two struggling kids new in marriage, trying to work extra jobs to get through college and make something of their lives. I learned firsthand life isn't always fair. Through the years, I found that when a friend or loved one is given the diagnosis of cancer I don't have to make a speech or say much to them. But my hand on their shoulder means more because they know I've been where they are.

Experiences like that did not make us bitter—but made us better. Brokenness from our hardship leads not to weakness but a different kind of strength. What we have experienced in our personal lives is the real source of true optimism and joy. Most cynics of the world have not experienced those life-altering moments, or if they have they failed to interpret them as opportunities for growth or strength but instead allowed them to become justifications for anger.

I would never want to go through something like that again with my wife. Through our thirty-two years of marriage there have been many other challenges for us; more than I could write in several volumes. But while I would never want to experience any of them again, I wouldn't trade anything for them either. Those experiences have helped me understand how deeply people can hurt, but also how much they can overcome. I cherish my moments on the mountaintop, because I've been to the depths of the valley.

Such experiences have served me well when I walk through the rubble of what was once a home, where a tornado has left little but splinters of wood and debris. I know that I cannot wave a magic wand and make all those possessions appear again, nor wipe away the pain and trauma that these dear people have experienced. It is not the time for platitudes or clichés. But I am able to look into their eyes and maybe share a hug and perhaps a tear, but also a smile to let them know that while all things material have indeed been lost, there remains hope.

The greatness of our nation is not in its government, its leaders, or its institutions. It is in the hopeful, optimistic spirit of its people. Their resilience has given them the ability to give life to this "experiment in government." From our beginning during a revolution for which we were ill-equipped and outmanned, and a "civil war" that divided the nation evenly in terms of geography and passion, we survived. Through wars that involved the entire planet and through great economic upheavals such as the Great Depression (which resulted in a collapse of the economic pillars and a massive migration of people from once strong and stable states to new frontiers), we have endured. We have witnessed the downfall, humiliation, and even assassination of our presidents. We have watched helplessly as our borders were violated in the horrific terrorist acts of September 11 in 2001. And we've rallied to help our fellow citizens overcome natural disasters ranging from hurricanes to tornadoes to floods and fires and earthquakes.

In spite of the cynics, trials, and losses we've faced, or perhaps because of the courage surviving them has given us, we have continued to be a people of hope.

12 Action Steps to STOP
Being Cynical

1. Don't believe bad reports without documentation.

2. Read the Bible more; blogs less.

3. Read more from the "Features" page and fewer from the "Letters to the Editor."

4. Listen to more music and less talk radio.

5. Watch classic films made before 1968.

6. Read biographies.

7. Read magazines about your favorite hobbies. (I read *Runner's World, Bassmaster, Ducks Unlimited, Men's Health,* and *Bass Player* for example, among others.)

8. Have regular conversations with people very unlike you (race, religion, political party, ethnic background).

9. Do volunteer work with the impoverished, disabled, or ill.

10. Write letters of praise to total strangers you read about who do wonderful things.

11. Practice what my Arkansas philanthropist friend Jennings Osborne calls "Random Acts of Kindness."

12. Watch TV Land and Nick @ Nite more; network TV less.

Chapter 2

STOP Thinking Horizontally

I'm a conservative, pro-life, pro-family evangelical who believes in God, lower taxes, less government, personal empowerment, personal ownership, and personal responsibility. I believe in the unlimited potential of the human spirit, a strong national defense, and a government that allows the marketplace to regulate itself as much as possible to encourage and enhance free enterprise. Despite partisan stereotypes, I'm not mad at everyone and my views are not driven by rage or even mild anger. Fact is, I'm a pretty happy guy most of the time. I have a simple philosophy—we need to take God more seriously and ourselves less seriously. Despite some tough times, my life has turned out far better than I deserve!

The political sphere is infected today with too many people who have lost a sense of humor and whose perspective is limited to the data stored in a single brain—their own. People are no longer political opponents, but true enemies. There is a growing desire not merely to win a political race or legislative battle but to disable or disfigure the opposition in a type of human demolition derby that has been described as the "politics of personal destruction."

Such tactics have not raised the level of public discourse or the quality of life in America, but have in fact imperiled our very system of government. The idea that citizens would run for or accept an appointed level of public service is losing ground as the risks are driven dramatically high that one will be investigated, indicted, or at the very least impaled on the spear of a determined reporter or political operative less interested in good government or good journalism than in winning an election or press prize.

It ought to be obvious that when a person's policies or position are not vulnerable, the only step left is to stoop to the lowest level of political practice and to engage in an attack on the person and his or her character, or worse, the family of the public figure.

I'm convinced that we are a nation that has grown weary of the *polarized* and *paralyzed* government that Americans are getting at a record cost. Too many in our nation's political ruling class think the only direction for us is to the left or to the right. I admit that I unapologetically lean right, but I think that the more important direction for the country (and the one the people of our nation are looking for) is not necessarily right or left.

We don't need our leadership to embrace a horizontal direction, but a vertical one—we need to aim *up*—not just right or left. This requires working toward something Washington can't seem to do—solve problems. Debate, discussions, and deliberations all have a place, but the ultimate purpose of the chatter is to make a *decision* and head in a clear direction. That direction doesn't have to always be an alienating right/left, win/lose, right/wrong. It can, and often should, be straight *up*.

Many issues that actually matter to folks sitting around the breakfast table are not about the politics of one side or the other. Mothers and fathers want good schools for their kids. Families want to live in safe neighborhoods. Small business entrepreneurs want at least a fighting chance to succeed. Motorists want fuel they can afford and the ability to drive on roads that are safe and in good shape. Everyone wants access to affordable health care when they are sick, and a job where they can earn a decent wage and not see most of it gobbled up in taxes wasted on irresponsible spending.

When government becomes so polarized and paralyzed that it's dysfunctional, the people no longer vote for leadership but feel forced to choose the lesser of evils. Their votes are cast based on the least amount of fear evoked from the thought of that person or party in charge. Did people vote *for* George W. Bush because they truly believed in his vision, or did they vote *against* John Kerry because they feared he stood for little, and was unpredictable and indecisive?

When polls showed the president's approval rating at an all-time low, they often failed to mention that Congress was even lower and that when Americans were asked if they favored Republican or Democrat, neither scored high enough on the trust factor to be above embarrassment.

Is there an option between vanilla and vanilla? Do we have to limit the hopes of America to bland choices that excite or inspire no one? Is it necessary to assume that our future will be established by ultimately electing leaders who survive the minefield that has become America's electoral system?

Let me admit something for the record: No one is right all the time and no one is wrong all the time. That's not politically correct and won't be appreciated by hard-liners, but it needs to be said.

There is value in approaching life with the attitude that I might actually learn something from those with whom I disagree. That's probably not the kind of view that gets featured on Jerry Springer. But it is far more representative of the American people and who *they* are than the extreme, arrogant, unyielding, and unproductive political spirit that permeates our climate today.

There are two powerful emotions that will motivate people—fear and hope.

Fear is an effective motivator and can activate strong actions in those who are afraid they will lose their health, job, house, comfort level, school, or freedom. Fear can evoke a miraculous response, such as the person who is suddenly able to lift a car off a friend due to the adrenaline rush in the midst of an accident. But fear has a short shelf life, and becomes hard to maintain as either the object of the fear doesn't materialize or if it does, a person learns to live with it and begins to react with more resolve.

Take, for example, a person given a diagnosis of cancer. Fear is overwhelming at first. The very word "cancer" evokes anxiety and panic. "Will I die? How much will it hurt? How long will I live?" These are just some of the immediate questions that spring to the surface of the mind as the doctor breaks the news. But in time, fear gives way to a fight-back mode, acceptance of what is deemed to be inevitable, or gives way to hope.

Hope motivates differently. More a slow burn than the explosion of fear, hope provides a sustained drive and determination for the long haul. It is the marathon instead of the sprint. Hope is that deeply rooted conviction that even after a hundred failures at trying to ride a bike, it's worth it to believe that the 101st attempt will be successful.

While fear is an event, hope is a process. Fear springs into action, but soon comes to exhaustion; hope stays active and endures.

In the days after September 11, Americans were frightened. Our fear brought us together and caused there to be a spirit of unity unlike any I had witnessed in my lifetime. Democrats joined Republicans to rally around the president and his call for action. Even Hollywood liberals were ready to launch bombs against the Taliban and Al-Qaeda. We responded to Code Orange.

When the anthrax scare happened, people were willing to tolerate a virtual suspension of civil liberties to make sure we nailed the bad guys.

Over time, however, the constant message of fear lost its punch. When we didn't get hit with another devastating terrorist attack, the regular warnings about Code Orange or Code Red no longer caused people to change travel plans, but instead became fodder for late-night comedy monologues. Fear had indeed brought America together for a short time, but fear could not sustain us as a nation. We will rise to our feet from fear, but it takes *hope* to keep us standing for the long term.

The next generation of political leadership will need to bring hope to the American people. Not that we will ignore the perils and personalities of terror or let our guard down as it relates to the multiple threats of Iran, North Korea, or the sleeper cells of extremists hell-bent on destroying our nation and killing vast numbers of our innocent citizens—but fear can only get us out of bed; it takes hope to get us through a good day's work.

When we are conflicted between our fears and our hopes, we lose focus, direction, and unity. As Americans returned to the routines they were used to prior to September 11, they rediscovered their old personalities, preferences, and partisanship. The failure was that when we stopped fearing, we didn't start hoping. Our leaders were unable to take us from the short run to the long run. We were not challenged to make any significant sacrifice and to work toward a different world, but were told, "Go about your regular routine; resume normalcy."

And we did!

If the "regular routine" meant that we would again divide along racial, economic, geographical, gender, religious, and political lines, then we were magnificently successful. Sadly, we didn't simply go back to business as usual but really allowed things to be business worse than usual.

On the evening of January 21, 1999, a tornado struck several parts of Arkansas, including the very grounds of the Governor's Mansion in Little Rock. I was attending a dinner one block away while my daughter, Sarah, was home alone. Her two older brothers were away at college and my wife was in Oklahoma for a speaking engagement.

It was the second time in my life I'd actually been in a tornado, the first time being when I was eleven years old. I had never forgotten that distinct trainlike sound nor the emptiness of the air just before it hit. As the tornado came upon us, I was mindful that this was no ordinary thunderstorm. As the tornado passed, the state trooper assigned to me helped make sure everyone was okay in the house we were in and then we tried to make our way back to the Governor's Mansion.

The Harvest Foods grocery store two hundred yards away was flattened. We would later discover that one of the employees there was killed, buried under the debris. Massive hardwood trees had been screwed out of the ground, leaving craters twenty feet wide and six feet deep. Trees blocked the streets, crushing cars and rooftops, and severing power lines. When we arrived home, the electronic gates to the compound of the mansion grounds were locked and the lack of power made it impossible to open them, so I climbed the fence. The sight of my daughter running out of the house unhurt was as precious as any I've seen. Meanwhile, in the streets, chaos reigned.

The area around the Governor's Mansion, called the Quapaw Quarter, is an eclectic one, with once stately old houses settled in among very expensive restored ones. Being a diverse neighborhood, people live near one another physically, if not socially or economically.

But on this particular night, people from the neighborhood poured into the streets to check on one another and assess the stunning damage of the F4 tornado. Whatever boundaries that had existed were no longer evident as the fences that had once separated properties were now on the ground, under the weight of the hundreds of massive trees that had been uprooted and tossed like toothpicks.

Disaster, danger, and crisis had brought the neighborhood together. In the weeks immediately afterward, as volunteers joined residents in helping clear the tons of debris, an unusual unity and sense of community took hold. The nicest homes had suffered just as had the not-so-restored rental properties. Many in the area were making decisions as to whether to fix things and stay or simply pack up what could be salvaged and relocate. It was a true neighborhood in those days with people talking, sharing, caring.

The significance of this was not lost on my wife or me. When we had first moved into the Governor's Mansion in July 1996, our arrival was not met with enthusiasm by most in the area. The Quapaw Quarter is overwhelmingly a Democratic neighborhood, as evidenced by the very few Republican votes recorded each election in our precinct. The arrival of a Republican interloper in the home that had been Bill and Hillary Clinton's for nearly twelve years before Tucker's three years in office was about as welcome as the tornado would be three years later. While a few of the neighbors spoke kindly and sought to make us feel at home (knowing that we were as surprised to be there as they were to have us), others were openly hostile.

Dozens of hate-filled letters were sent anonymously; others, proudly signed, proclaimed that we lacked the "class" to live in such a fine and stately home, and expressed fear that we would destroy the dignity of the historic structure. My wife was viciously attacked for everything from the manner in which the azaleas were trimmed to the fact that we had made the Governor's Mansion smoke-free and removed alcoholic beverages. It was, after all, not only an event center but also the home where we and our teenage children would reside. One would have thought that we had turned off the water, put old cars on concrete blocks on the front lawn, hung laundry on the fence, and raised chickens and hogs in the backyard!

The spirit of things in the immediate days after the tornado created quite a different atmosphere. People who had never spoken to us did so for the first time, and we actually got smiles from some who had literally turned the other way previously as they had walked dogs past the property.

There was especially a sense of relief when we publicly announced that we had decided against relocating the Governor's Mansion to another part of town. We planned to do our best to restore things to a "better than before" condition to help provide an anchor for the neighborhood and its beautiful and historic homes so others would rebuild and restore their damaged homes to an even better condition. If the decision had been made for the Governor's Mansion to abandon the area, it would have dealt a crippling blow to what had been, and should remain, a wonderful residential treasure of unique and carefully crafted homes, many of which are over a hundred years old and had been home to some of the state's early leaders.

Major renovations were done to the property, including a total update of wiring, plumbing, and infrastructure, but also an expensive, but very necessary move to make the entire property compliant with ADA (Americans with Disabilities Act). We felt that the "People's House," should be accessible *to all* the people. We were personally aghast when disabled people were unable to enjoy a visit to the Governor's Mansion due to numerous impediments. Part of the limited family living space had to be given up, but it was well worth it to have a facility in which wheelchair-bound guests were not humiliated by being manhandled down stairs to simply use the restroom.

Plans for the Grand Hall, a banquet room for larger public events, had been discussed for over a decade, but nothing had been done to start the project. My wife led the efforts to raise private funds for the construction of the Grand Hall and a complete makeover of the nearly nine acres of property to make it more accessible, attractive, and functional. For the first time, we started feeling like a welcome part of the neighborhood.

Then came the elections of 2002, in which I was up for reelection. I didn't expect neighborhood rallies for us, given the long-standing political leanings of most of the residents, but some of the expressions were sheer excess. One neighbor actually put out not one, nor two, but *seven* yard signs for my opponent in the front lawn of his home. Others put two or three. It became comical to us to see how far some would go to express their hope that we'd be packing up and moving out in January 2003. I was convinced that if defeated, we would have plenty of offers to help us move out!

Politics had replaced the pleasant but short-lived politeness that we had experienced in the days following the tornado and efforts to improve the property. I was reminded that for some people, it's easier to keep old prejudices and partisan peeves than to be able to show some level of civility.

America is a land of good and decent people, and they show their best in the midst of common peril. But in times of prosperity, peace, and power, we can be at our worst, allowing the petty and the puny to overwhelm our deeply stored decency.

Even within the confines of one's own political family, there can be mean-spiritedness. Some of the most hostile things said to (but more often about) me have come from those who claim and proclaim that they *are more* conservative than I am and their particular and self-proclaimed brand of conservatism is more *pure* than mine.

I'm convinced that many of the divisions we have are not due to our true convictions or principles but to the need to preserve one's artificial sense of superiority and the innate insecurity that results in a wall erected, instead of a bridge built. Some fear getting too close to someone who is different. It causes discomfort for those so insecure in their views or values that it's more comfortable to keep a distance and hold to the prejudice than to engage in a conversation and discover that while differences are real, dialogue and discussion is actually desirable.

The basic human condition that separates people is *pride*. I once heard an eloquent African-American pastor speak of the four kinds of pride: *pride of face* (outward appearance); *pride of place* (socioeconomic position); *pride of race* (ethnic background); and *pride of grace* (religion). Most of the angry, spiteful, hateful, and vitriolic spirits of the day are really manifestations of some form of *selfish pride* as described above.

I'm not suggesting that we ignore our deeply held political, religious, or patriotic positions and engage in a group hug, build a campfire, toast marshmallows, and sing "Kum Ba Yah." But I am saying that much of the rage that fills the air of America today is not about principles but old-fashioned and ill-aimed prejudice and pride. It is America at its worst and we can do better. In fact, I believe that the next generation of young Americans needs to lead a new American spirit. They need to demonstrate the will to engage in spirited debate and build relationships with people who may not look like, think like, eat like, speak like, celebrate like, or worship like they do.

Is it not possible for people to have different points of view and discuss them at less than a shouting level? There are indeed moments when anger ought to be a part of our reaction, such as when a child is molested or a woman is savagely brutalized by an acquaintance or husband. It ought to make us mad when some white-collar corporate crook lives like an emperor while spending the last penny in the pension accounts of the working stiffs who actually earned the company wealth he is squandering. We should be outraged when a young, poor, black male gets a longer sentence for being caught with an ounce of marijuana, while the affluent white male from the nice neighborhood gets probation and a few months of counseling for having multiple prescriptions for a painkiller. We ought to be angry that children in our own nation will go to bed hungry tonight, and that some families will live in substandard housing that doesn't even provide running water or a warm place to sleep.

The extremes of the left and right need to give way to the mainstream of American goodness. Leadership is not about getting behind people and kicking them in the rear but getting in front to model the behavior of service and sacrifice.

The brilliantly written script of *The Manchurian Candidate*—a classic movie originally released during the height of the Cold War with a recent modernized (but less compelling) remake—provides a simple but profound truth that illustrates this point. The most extreme version on the left and the most extreme version on the right go so far from the top of the circle that they end up joining at the bottom of the circle. We see much of this today, with the common ground being name-calling, personal attacks, and venomous and vicious assaults on political figures, their families, their physical features, or even their faith.

Coarse language, once heard only in rare moments of elevated anger, is now part of the everyday vernacular of many Americans, especially the younger generations. Movies and song lyrics routinely add profanity as if it were a stutter or an expression of "uh." An AP-Ipsos poll revealed that nearly 80 percent of Americans reported encountering profanity with regularity, and 62 percent of eighteen to thirty-four-year-olds confessed to using profanity in ordinary conversation several times a week, compared to only 39 percent of men age thirty-five and older. It's been said that profanity is the strong expression of a weak mind. The excessive use of such language causes it to lose any impact or shock value, and only demonstrates disrespect and contempt for others and for propriety.

We can do better and we must do better. America is not putting on its best face when it wears anger on its sleeve. We do best when we exhibit compassion and kindness. We are not hindered by spirited debate or even stark disagreement. Such differences give traction to our policies and tenacity to our policymakers. But we need to be driven by something far more powerful and effective than petty and selfish rage. Warm hearts produce better results than hot heads, and our government policies need to reflect how people are affected instead of how purses are affected.

12 Action Steps to STOP Thinking Horizontally

1. Open doors for others.
2. Tip waiters and waitresses generously.
3. Attend worship services every week.
4. Compliment a co-worker.
5. Always say "Thank you."
6. Know the name of the person who cleans your office building.
7. Never ask for anything without saying "Please."
8. Don't use profanity.
9. Just for the fun of it, allow someone behind you in the checkout line to go first.
10. If you see a parent and a child together at a ball game, shopping, or a park, say, "It just does my heart good to see a parent spend time with his/her child."
11. Always pull over to the side of the road when a funeral procession approaches, and once a year, visit a cemetery and read the headstones.
12. Purchase some inexpensive umbrellas and give them to total strangers on a rainy day.

Chapter 3

STOP CHEATING OUR CHILDREN

When I am asked my reasons for getting into politics, I often say I had three—John Mark, David, and Sarah, my children. It is fair to say that I was genuinely motivated as I saw their world being changed by public officials—many of whom seemed to be clueless as to what living in the real world with the rest of us hoi polloi was all about. This was especially true as it related to policies of public education.

Education funding is far and away the most costly part of the Arkansas general revenue budget, which I oversaw for ten and a half years as governor. When combined with higher education, our general revenue expenses in education are approximately 70 percent of the total state budget.

Every elected official claims to care deeply about public education and promises to take steps to reform it. One cannot imagine a campaign whose theme was "elect me and I will leave our schools just like they are, with the same process and the same results."

It has also been interesting to me that while many elected officials pontificate proudly about their deep interest in and commitment to public education, so many put their own children in private schools. If the public schools are so deserving of their (and our) support, why aren't they deserving of the *ultimate* support—having confidence enough in them for their own children to be educated there?

My three children were the first children of any Arkansas governor in at least fifty years who spent their first through senior high education entirely in the public schools of Arkansas.

My wife and I are ourselves products of public schools. For us, there was no other option as we grew up in families that could not have afforded a private school had one even existed in our hometown. From my earliest days, my parents placed an extraordinary and urgent sense of value on education for my older sister and me. They drilled deeply in me the idea that education was essential to my future and that I should seek to take advantage of the learning opportunities that would be before me. They insisted that I study, complete my homework, make good grades, and do my best academically. Frankly, I could have done better at the high school level, but I was involved in extracurricular activities such as the Student Council, theater, and my work schedule at the local radio station. At the time I didn't see any particular need in going beyond what I was already doing.

No male in my family for as far back as I can trace the family tree had ever even graduated from high school, much less attended college. My mother had graduated from high school, but as the oldest of seven children she was forced to go to work to help with her younger brothers and sisters. She and my father pretty well insisted that my sister and I do well in school and get a college education so our opportunities would extend beyond any they had known.

I was fortunate to attend public schools in Hope. While far from perfect, and terribly underfunded by today's standards, my teachers instilled in me a love of learning and constantly challenged me to dream big dreams and to always follow the instincts of my curiosity.

As governor, although the teachers' union in Arkansas never supported me (mainly because they have so long been controlled by the machinery of the Democratic Party), improving education in the public schools has understandably been a priority for me.

In 1998 I announced an initiative we called Smart Start, the first of several major reform efforts in Arkansas that were to focus on not only increased funding but, more important, improved results. Later the K–4 Smart Start Initiative would be joined by Smart Step, which took the Smart Start principles to grades five through eight. Ultimately we launched Next Step, which was the full implementation of a reform strategy that included grades nine through twelve.

It was a priority for me to develop more accessible and effective preschool programs and to make dramatic changes in both access and affordability in higher education. We developed a seamless curriculum from pre-K through college so that there was coordination and continuity throughout the educational process. The previous approach had often been completely disjointed, and compartmentalized the many aspects of the educational system. Both parents and employers should insist that politicians quit merely talking about reform and provide true examples of how to make this expensive, but crucial government expenditure a good bang for their buck.

There are at least five elements essential to improving schools and significant results leading to real hope for America's students:

Mark the Standards

With the launching of Smart Start, we raised the standards dramatically rather than lower them and artificially claim greater success. A goal that isn't challenging is a goal not worth reaching. Education reform involves raising standards and making sure they are consistent with those being established in other states as well as in other nations.

Whether in athletics, business, or academics, improvement comes by performing against a challenging and demanding standard, not by lowering expectations to create the false illusion of success.

Making sure that the standards are not only challenging but consistent from school to school and district to district is crucial. Imagine how difficult it would be if every school that played basketball individually decided how high the rim would be from the floor, and had their own standard of distance from one end of the court to the other. Chaos would ensue when any team played another. Setting standards is absolutely critical. Those standards must be challenging but they also must have consistency, otherwise they are meaningless.

In my first few years in office we laid the foundation for many reforms related to genuine standards, including:

- Criminal background checks for teachers.
- Character education incorporated into the school curriculum to teach good manners and basic elements of personal character and honor.
- A single-track core curriculum, which stopped the previous process of directing students in the eighth grade toward either a college track or a vocational track. I found it particularly troubling to have a system in which kids were marked by the government toward a future based on the subjective opinions of either teachers or counselors. Adolescents are in no position to be making permanent life decisions, and are more conflicted about what to wear to the mall than what career choice might lie in their future!
- School report cards that give parents and taxpayers an opportunity to see their child's individual performance and a report card on the school itself.
- National Board Teacher Certification incentives to encourage teachers to develop their skills. The National Board Teaching Certificate is a challenging professional advancement program and one of the most effective enrichment tools for American educators. We not only encourage teachers to participate but give them up to $5,000 additional salary for board certification, plus full reimbursement on the cost of becoming certified. We found it was in our best interest to encourage the level of excellence that came from the demanding process of National Board Certification.
- The Fair Dismissal Law addressing the issue of school boards and superintendents being blocked from removing incompetent teachers due to union-led impediments. The Fair Dismissal Act provided adequate protection to a teacher for being unfairly terminated, but finally gave school administrators the power of ensuring that teachers were professionally competent and personally responsible for their behavior.
- The authorization and advancement of charter schools. I have long advocated that charter schools are wonderful laboratories for education reform. Critics often claim that many charter schools fail, but that is precisely the point of a charter school and its difference from a traditional one. In a charter school, if it doesn't succeed in meeting its agreed-upon goals, we simply close it. Traditional public schools have failed for generations to adequately educate students, but they keep getting funded year

after year. Charter schools can bring innovative ideas to the marketplace with little long-term financial risk.

Measure the Progress

It is important to have standards but unless we are measuring how well we are doing against those standards, little if any progress can be made. The bipartisan breakthrough education effort pushed by President Bush in 2001 called No Child Left Behind has often been marked by controversy, but it truly represents one of the most significant reforms in American education. Its critics have alleged that it is underfunded or that it raises unrealistic expectations of every child succeeding. The reality is that it has forced schools to improve or close. For the first time we have shone the light on the actual effectiveness of schools and given real empowerment to parents to get their children in schools that are both efficient and competent.

A major complaint about No Child Left Behind or any reform effort is that there is too much testing. One sometimes hears the lament that teachers are merely "teaching to the test." While that sounds like a convincing argument at first, it is utter nonsense to suggest that we should not have fair and comprehensive testing to see how well students are actually performing against the standards that have been set. Testing students is the equivalent of keeping score when two sports teams play. Can anyone imagine going to an interscholastic high school basketball game and having the official turn off the scoreboard and announce to the crowd that the score will not be kept because it is not important? "We don't want these athletes to score points; we want them to play so as to enjoy the experience in the gymnasium and have the health benefit of running up and down the court in front of the fans."

It is equally absurd to suggest that we should be spending billions of dollars on education in America and not have a scoreboard to see how well the students are doing. We need to know how well they are performing against the standards established by the state for that state, and also how well they are performing compared to students across the nation and across the world.

Since we *raised* the standards in Arkansas and started keeping careful score, we have seen significant improvement in every level tested in each year, and have noted the most significant actual gains in student performance in the history of the state. An example of the results can be found in the fourth grade literacy and math scores. Since 1998, when we instituted Smart Start, the percentage of students at the proficient level or advanced level has increased from 37 percent steadily to 69 percent. In fourth grade math the percentage of students in the proficient or advanced level went from 31 percent to 65 percent during a seven-year period. Similar results were seen at the sixth grade, eighth grade, and at end-of-the-year tests in algebra, geometry, and eleventh grade literacy.

Along with significantly rising test scores, we have also dramatically increased teacher pay by an average of $10,000 per year, moving Arkansas from near the bottom of the list in terms of salary to being one of the most competitive states in our region. When considering the lower cost of living in our state, our salaries rank in the top fifteen nationally.

Meet the Expectations

There must also be accountability for the results so that stakeholders know that there is more on the line than the mere pride of better performance. In every endeavor there is accountability for how well a job is done except in traditional public education. Historically Americans have viewed education in terms of being a *process* rather than a system measured by actual *progress*.

Accountability must mean more than simply having the power to fire teachers whose students do not improve. Accountability must extend to the students themselves, for if test scores have no impact upon the student, the student will not be inclined to take testing seriously. A friend of mine who was a high school football coach once made the observation, "How would you like for your job to depend upon the performance on any given Friday night of a bunch of seventeen-year-old kids?"

There are three key elements to real accountability we have attempted to implement in Arkansas that should be a part of any genuine education reform: *transparency*, *efficiency*, and *responsibility*.

Transparency means it doesn't take an accounting degree to understand how money is being spent, by whom, and for what purpose.

Efficiency in how taxpayer money is spent ensures that the bulk of the money is actually getting into the classroom and not gobbled up by administration, competitive athletics, or frills in facilities.

Responsibility makes those responsible for a task accountable for that task.

One of the most important pieces of legislation passed in Arkansas to achieve educational reform was a bill from the 2003 legislative session commonly referred to as the Omnibus Education Act. This bill empowered the state board of education to do more than issue warnings to underperforming schools, it gave them the authority to step in after two consecutive years of fiscal or academic distress and, when appropriate, terminate the superintendent, fire and replace the entire school board, and assume all operations of the failing school. While a drastic measure, it is inexcusable that schools which fail to efficiently, properly, or adequately spend taxpayer money continue to exist year after year. Those responsible for such mismanagement should be held accountable. Only in public education have we typically allowed total failure to result in continued employment and automatic annual pay raises!

There were some things in Arkansas I was unable to convince the legislature to do, mainly because the ideas were politically charged with great risk and controversy. I had hoped that we would pass legislation that would have restricted the total amount a school district could spend on administration to no more than 8 percent. I further had hoped that we would insist on following reasonable economies of scale as related to the size of a school district. We had some school districts in which the entire student population in grades K–12 was as few as 112 students, yet we still employed a superintendent and administrative staff. This resulted in huge inefficiencies at the administrative level at the expense of classroom expenditures. We made progress, but not as much as we could and should have.

Mobilize the Community

Schools don't exist in a vacuum, and good schools are usually the result of having excellent teachers and adequate resources, as well as an involved and mobilized community that sees education as an important and essential foundation for everyone's quality of life.

I will never forget the town hall meeting in North Arkansas at a time when I was pressing the need for improving public schools through higher standards, tough testing, and strong accountability. A lady in the audience raised her hand. When I called on her, she proceeded to emphatically tell me that she was not the least bit interested in spending another dime on public education. Her kids were out of school and on their own, so she did not feel it was her responsibility to be interested in the public schools any longer. In her view, the only value of public schools was to educate *her* children.

I was stunned by her total disconnect with the value of a competent education system. While not politically correct, I challenged her that it should matter to her what kind of schools we have. I reminded her that on a hot August day her air conditioner might go out and she would find it necessary to call a service technician; someday when she was driving after dark on a deserted road her car might break down requiring the services of a mechanic; and while I hoped it not to be the case, there could come a time when she would be stretched out on an operating table with her life on the line. I reminded her that the person repairing her air conditioner, her automobile, or handing the instruments to her surgeon is probably a product of the public education system.

While it might not matter to her, I told her that it certainly mattered to me that the people I dealt with were competent enough to make change, fix things when they are broken, and have the capacity to read and write at a level that gives them the professional skills that I might need and that would power our local economy.

Schools cannot be substitutes for the roles and responsibilities of moms and dads. Too many parents want to treat their children like they would treat dry cleaning—dropping them off at school in the morning and picking them up in the afternoon with the expectation that they will be well fed, well educated, and well exercised.

For American schools to be at their best, mothers and fathers need to be involved in ensuring that their children are studying and completing their homework. They need to know their children are enrolled in the classes that help them to excel.

Further, good schools must involve parents and members of the business community to make sure students are preparing for jobs that are actually going to exist. Kids can't be educated in a vacuum.

While speaking to a large civic club with several hundred people in attendance, consisting primarily of business owners and employers, I posed this question: "How many of you could operate your businesses if everyone in your workforce had nothing more than a high school diploma?" Not a single hand went up. To make sure that they understood, I asked the question again. Once more, not a single hand went up.

Today an education is no longer K–12 but at a bare minimum K–14, which means that beyond a high school diploma, students will need specialized training in order to be a plumber, automotive technician, or electrician. They may opt to get a four-year degree or more and become a physicist, teacher, or pharmacist. One of the reasons that we cannot afford to waste a single day of a student's education is because we must ensure that the curriculum throughout the student's career prepares him or her for a future that will actually exist.

For two years I served as chairman of the Education Commission of the States, a consortium of governors, legislators, and education chiefs from each of the fifty states. It has existed for over forty years to advance education policy and conduct research on effective trends in education.

One of the studies the commission conducted was to determine the most important factors in predicting whether a student would succeed in college. When I have posed the question to audiences, most respondents guess that the key predictors would be socioeconomic standing or even race in determining the likelihood a student would complete college. Both of these responses are quite wrong. Fifty years of research indicates that the key predictor of getting through college and graduating is having access to and participation in a rigorous and challenging curriculum at the high school level. It is critical that schools offer a broad range of courses and that the rigor of the curriculum is challenging, adequately preparing the student for a real future.

Move the Potential

We live in a very different kind of world that requires a very different kind of academic preparation. Students no longer compete against the students across town, across the state, or even across the country. They are competing with students around the world in the emerging economies of China and India as well as Europe.

Ninety percent of CEOs surveyed said that attracting and retaining talented people is their top priority and their greatest challenge. Job seekers need to have more than an education—they need critical thinking and the ability to come up with creative solutions. The development of such skills is connected to a glaring error being committed by many practitioners of public policy in education.

We will never move the potential of our students to its full capacity if we cheat them out of a *complete* education, which includes art and music. The economy of the future is likely to be based on different models than past ones like physical strength and a strong back. It won't even be based on mere intellectual capacity. The key is *creative capacity*. Richard Florida's landmark book *The Rise of the Creative Class* creates a portrait of the American workforce as one in which creativity rules not only the marketplace of jobs but also has a dramatic impact on where people choose to live.

Unlike my baby boomer generation, the Gen X generation is not driven as much by money and materialism and individuals often make career decisions based on opportunities for personal lifestyle choices such as availability of local theater, art, music, or recreation. People choose careers and communities with a focus on quality of life as much as quantity of salary.

From an educational standpoint, numerous studies have shown a direct correlation between music education and math scores. This makes perfect sense in that the study of music helps develop both the left and right sides of the brain and improves spatial reasoning and the capacity to think in the abstract. In other words, the basic fundamental values one employs to learn music can be applied to learning any other discipline. A person learns how to learn, and that skill is transferable in learning foreign languages, algebra, or history. The younger the age at which one is exposed to and learns music, the more impact the study of music will have on his or her academic capacity and achievement.

Music is a part of who we are from our very creation. It is in our God-given nature to be musically inclined. The first rhythm we are exposed to is the heartbeat in our mother's womb. From almost the moment we are born and throughout infancy we are exposed to parents and caregivers who instinctively sing to us and communicate their affection and information such as the alphabet through music. Children are soothed by music, and the familiar refrains of a lullaby are as comforting to a child as food.

Sadly, as the child grows older, decisions are made for him or her by school budget officers who often determine that a music program is too expensive. I argue that it is too expensive to the future of the child to *not* have music! Although there are clear academic benefits, we need to be cautious in assuming that the purpose of music and arts curriculum is as some associated or secondary value in other academic disciplines. There is value in music and the arts on their own merits, and not everything we study has to have a finite result of some type of productivity to have intrinsic value and worth.

One of the pieces of legislation of which I am most proud requires every student in Arkansas schools to receive established time in both music and the arts taught by a certified teacher. I still remember the battle not only over the subject matter but the necessity of having music and art taught by competent teachers who are actually trained and fully certified in their fields. I was stunned when a legislator arguing against the need for certified teachers in these fields said, "Anybody can teach music; all you have to do is play a recording." I replied, "That attitude is *exactly* why we *need* the certified teachers!"

Because of tight budgeting, some school districts make the tragic mistake of believing that music and arts programs are simply too expensive. I would argue that music and art are not expendable, they are not extracurricular, and they are not extraneous. They are essential!

Despite the determination of some to exclude a music and arts curriculum on the basis of it not being a vital part of a student's preparation, some 1.7 million people called themselves artists in 1990 as opposed to 400,000 in 1950. The growing number of people who consider themselves artists is an affirmation that even when some supposed educational experts put it on the chopping block, there is still a yearning deep within the hearts and souls of human beings to express themselves and to carry the message of a culture from one generation to the next through the vital, necessary, and treasured forms of art and music.

I would contend that the attempt to cut the arts in a school system is about the dumbest move a school board or superintendent could make. Political officials might be interested to know that nine of ten parents *oppose* cuts in an arts program. Not only is it *right*—but it is politically *smart* to insist on continuing, if not expanding, music and arts programs for every student in America!

We must ensure that "no child is left behind." But many children will be left behind if the only talents we touch are those of the mathematicians or the athletes. The talents of the actor, the musician, the singer, the painter, or the dancer are as important as the talent of the young aspiring scientist. Beyond the intrinsic value of music and art is the tremendous inspiration and motivation they provide to many students.

The arts have value in teaching patience, perseverance, and the power of practice toward personal performance. One learns that for every minute on stage, there are hours and hours behind the scenes in rehearsal. The power of cooperation and teamwork also is a benefit to music and the arts, and students learn that without the set designers, stagehands, sound and lighting technicians, and makeup artists, the actors would have a dark, empty, lifeless stage and the curtain would never open. Both direct and indirect benefits make the arts a necessity for a total education.

In 1966 an eleven-year-old kid begged his parents for an electric guitar for Christmas. The eleven-year-old was absorbed in the music of the era—the Beatles and other rock bands—and wanted to play the electric guitar. He promised to faithfully practice and learn to play if he were to get the guitar for Christmas. The cost of an electric guitar, even one purchased through the J. C. Penney catalog, was well beyond the budget of a family struggling to make the rent payment by the first of each month. Somehow those parents made sacrifices and arrangements to make monthly payments over a year for the guitar and a small amplifier, which cost a total of $99.

The boy practiced for hours on end, often playing until his fingers were near bleeding. Like many other kids of his generation, he formed a rock band while still in junior high school and continued to play throughout his student days in various venues ranging from high school dances to small shows in school auditoriums.

As you read this you probably think that this is the story of a young, aspiring guitarist who would go on to a lucrative career as a famous musician and entertainer, but it didn't work out quite that way. He never made it as a professional rock and roll musician, but while turning to other endeavors he never quite got music out of his system either. He is now past the age of fifty, but he claims to enjoy it more than ever. He plays in a rock band made up of people who all have other day jobs but now play for the fun of it. His band opened for Willie Nelson in a sold-out nine-thousand-seat arena, as well as the Charlie Daniels Band, Grand Funk Railroad, Dionne Warwick, 38 Special, and Percy Sledge. He has played in venues ranging from presidential inauguration parties to the famous Red Rocks Amphitheatre in Denver, and a concert at the foot of the Brooklyn Bridge in New York.

By the way, that eleven-year-old kid who begged for the guitar is the author of this book who still loves music and whose band Capitol Offense has helped keep him sane through many challenges of raising a family and swimming in political waters!

Every student should have the opportunity to explore their creative abilities, whether it's by joining a band, acting in a play, or singing in a church choir. While most people cannot play tackle football at my age, there is never an age in which we will outgrow the ability to appreciate as well as to participate in music and the arts. They are truly endeavors that can be enjoyed for a lifetime.

Insistence on music and art for every student in America could well be one of the issues on which Republicans and Democrats could agree. Sadly, education has also become a battleground for Republicans and Democrats to take sides; for urban and rural interests to take sides; for unions and management to take sides; for parents and teachers to take sides; for administrators and faculty to take sides; and for the public and private sectors to take sides.

I have spent time in India, Taiwan, Korea, and Japan, all of which have growing and expanding economies. Some, such as Korea and Taiwan, have experienced nothing short of miraculous evolutions during the past twenty-five years toward high per capita income, booming economies, and substantial increases in personal freedom and democracies. In each case, I have asked government officials from those countries what has caused the dramatic change from impoverished and almost primitive agricultural economies to world leaders. In every case without exception, the answer was *education*. In America, we need to demand that we judge the true success of our education system by the results we obtain instead of the revenues we spend. The focus on true quality instead of mere quantity requires us to set high standards, measure performance diligently, and hold stakeholders accountable for the results in an atmosphere of transparency and efficiency.

12 Action Steps to STOP Cheating Our Children

1. If you are a parent, attend PTA and parent-teacher conferences.

2. Never miss a musical performance or school play your child is involved in.

3. Volunteer to help out in at least one school activity a year.

4. Attend a school board meeting (careful—you might be tempted to run for school board!).

5. Know your child's school test scores in comparison to other schools in the community, state, and nation.

6. Know how much your district spends per student in education.

7. Know how much teachers, coaches, principals, and superintendents are paid.

8. Ask the local school district for a breakdown of the school budget—administration, athletics, academics, and the arts.

9. Find out how serious your school is about the arts (classes required; offered; requirement to have certified teachers).

10. Ask for test scores of a class over a five-year period—are the scores stagnant, declining, improving?

11. Visit a private or parochial school and ask about their expenditures vs. public school expenditures.

12. Talk to your state legislator and let him or her know your interest in their voting record for education.

Chapter 4

STOP THE CULTURE OF CHRONIC DISEASE

March 6, 2005, is a day that will be as memorable to me as the date of my marriage and the birthdays of my children. It is the day that four hours and thirty-eight minutes after the sound of the starting gun, I crossed the finish line. I had completed 26.2 miles in the Little Rock Marathon.

Three years earlier, running a marathon seemed as likely to me as piloting the Space Shuttle or performing brain surgery. But back then there had also been 110 pounds more of me! After I was freshly diagnosed as a type 2 diabetic, my doctor had sat me down and told me that without a lifestyle change, I would be dead within a decade. The news propelled me on a life-changing and life-saving pilgrimage that eventually led to the achievement of something I would have thought unreasonable for a once nonathletic "sofa spud" like me. When people ask about the experience, I tell them that running the marathon was not difficult; in fact, the day of the marathon was a day of sheer ecstasy and pleasure. But the discipline to prepare for the event was as challenging as anything I've ever done.

I had endured seven months of intense training, rising early in the morning to go on solitary runs before daylight. On weekends, I would devote an escalating amount of time to increasing distances, leading up to a twenty-mile run three weeks before the actual event. When I ran the marathon, I had the bonus of cheering crowds, and runners in front, behind, and on either side, so the entire journey was sparked by a flow of adrenaline. The crowded streets during the marathon contrasted greatly to the lonely miles on rural highways in Pike County in the Ouachita Mountains.

My own personal experience is characteristic of our nation as a whole. We are a nation marked by serious chronic illness, and we are long past the crisis stage. Seventy-five percent of America's health care costs are due to chronic disease. And chronic disease is what causes people to limp and crawl to the finish line of life instead of getting to the finish line still on the go. Over 80 percent of a person's lifetime health care expenses are incurred in the last eighteen months of life—mostly due to the effects of chronic disease.

Approximately 700,000 people will die in America this year due to the effects of eating too much, exercising too little, and smoking tobacco products. If two thousand Americans died in the collapse of a building, or from the effects of a national disaster or a terrorist attack, our nation would be shocked to its knees. But imagine if two thousand people died today, and another two thousand tomorrow, and the day after that, and kept dying at a growing rate through the course of a year. That is exactly what is happening today with the impact of self-inflicted chronic disease. It is not only killing vast numbers of our population but leaving many others disabled, debilitated, and debt-ridden for life.

The health care system in this nation is irreparably broken, in part because it is only a "health care" system. We have failed to create a "*health system.*" We focus on raising and spending enormous amounts of money to treat chronic diseases, but seem oblivious to the urgent need to focus on the prevention of those diseases.

The system itself is in part to blame—doctors, hospitals, drug companies, and other providers do not get reimbursed for people being well, but rather for treating people who are sick. Most government grants are given to research for treatment of disease and to find ways to aggressively treat illnesses, or even to mask their effects. Preventive medicine, until recently, was almost considered a form of quackery. The late Dr. Fay Boozman, director of the Arkansas Department of Health during my tenure as governor, and for whom the Dr. Fay Boozman College of Public Health was named, used to say, "We are treating snakebites when we need to be killing snakes."

In order to confront the culture of chronic disease, we first must address *what* the crisis is, then *why* it exists, and finally *how* we can practically and effectively address it.

What — Defining the Crisis

Since 1990, there has been a 77 percent increase in obesity. Over 25 percent of Americans are considered inactive, and an alarming 65 percent are overweight. I once heard the American population compared to the scene at an NFL football game, where twenty-two men on the field desperately need rest while the sixty thousand people in the stands watching them desperately need exercise.

Just fifteen years ago, type 2 diabetes in preteens was almost non-existent. It was even called "adult onset diabetes" because it occurred only in adults. Large pediatric hospitals like Arkansas Children's Hospital had never seen a case of type 2 diabetes in a preteen. Today, that same medical facility and teaching hospital diagnoses a dozen cases a week of children as young as eight or nine years old with type 2 diabetes. A child developing diabetes at that young age is sure to have vision problems in his twenties, a heart attack before he is thirty, renal failure and full kidney dialysis by the time he is forty, and will be dead before he is fifty. Without a significant direction change, kids born today will be the first generation of young Americans that will not live as long as their parents and grandparents!

According to the Centers for Disease Control, approximately $35 billion a year is spent on disease costs directly related to diet alone, and another $9 billion is attributed to the lack of productivity. The cost of smoking adds $116 a month to a person's health care expenses.

At the turn of the past century, the greatest causes of death among Americans were infectious diseases such as smallpox, malaria, yellow fever, or influenza. The development of vaccines, better hygiene habits, insect control, and attention to prevention led to these diseases posing virtually no threat to the health or life of the American population today.

In the twenty-first century, we face a greater threat than ever before: Americans are dying in record numbers from heart disease, complications of diabetes, cancer, and a long list of ailments that are largely lifestyle-induced and, for the most part, preventable. An American who maintains normal body weight, eats healthy nutritious food, and refrains from smoking is likely to live thirteen years longer than one who engages in bad health habits.

In economic terms, U.S. citizens spend 53 percent more than the people of any other country on health care costs. The growth in that spending continues at approximately twice the rate of inflation. In 2004, health care spending in the United States climbed to close to $2 trillion, which worked out to approximately $6,300 per person. Even more frightening is the fact that health care spending now consumes almost 17 percent of our nation's gross domestic product. At the current rate of growth, it is estimated that a full 20 percent of our GDP will be allocated toward health care costs alone by the year 2015. No nation on earth spends 17 percent of their GDP on health care. In fact, only a few countries in Europe spend close to 10 percent. If Americans were spending even 11 percent of their GDP on health care instead of the current 17 percent, the annual savings to the nation would be over $700 billion! If we are able to steer this country toward healthy habits, we will also steer this country toward a healthier economy.

Why—The Cause for the Dilemma

In the spring of 2006, the U.S. Coast Guard recommended that operators of small boats raise the weight estimates for passengers because Americans are much fatter than when the first standards were issued in 1942. In 2004, five people were killed when a water taxi capsized in Baltimore. The operator had assumed the average person weighed 140 pounds, per the old Coast Guard standards, but the Centers for Disease Control now estimates that the average American weighs 178 pounds without clothing, so the new standard is 185 pounds.

And we're still getting bigger generation by generation. If you are twenty-five years old or older, look through your personal belongings and find an old scrapbook or school yearbook from the third grade. Take a good look at your third grade class, then walk into any third grade class today and tell me what you immediately notice. I'm sure the contrasts of sizes between the students today and your third grade class will be significant.

Some have opined that childhood obesity can be blamed on changes in our education system. Ridding schools of vending machines and adding physical education classes is the best way to resolve the issue. Yet studies from the University of North Carolina showed that an adolescent gets only about 2 percent of his or her total calories from all vending machines combined, not just those at school. As far as physical education, good health habits are more "caught" than taught. Part of the problem lies with children who see poor health habits practiced by their parents and accept such practices as normal.

Meanwhile, at the government level, most politicians focus only on a discussion of "health care"—how to access it and how to afford it—but such a discussion is missing the greater issue. How do we change the "culture of health" in America from one that focuses on disease to one that focuses on health and wellness? Of course, part of the reason that politicians love to talk about health care is because it empowers them to come up with solutions to solve the problem. The assumption that this is primarily a function of government is a fundamental mistake. While government certainly has a role to play, and a significant one, it cannot be the "Sugar Sheriff" or act as the "Grease Police." Warren Buffett once said, "Never ask your barber if you need a haircut." For sure, never ask a politician if we need a greater government program because the answer will inevitably be yes.

While government can't force us to begin living healthy lifestyles, it must first acknowledge that it has contributed to the unhealthy lifestyles that now kill us in record numbers.

Many people addicted to nicotine and ultimately killed by tobacco had their first taste of it courtesy of the United States government, which subsidized the growing of the product, encouraged the manufacturing of tobacco into cigarettes by way of economic incentives, and then distributed the product as if it were life-saving food! The fact that the government handed out cigarettes to young soldiers as part of the war rations in World War II, Korea, and Vietnam seems insane now, but was accepted policy for decades.

Today, that same government encourages the serving of mass amounts of unhealthy trans fats and high fructose corn syrup in government commodities passed on to our poorest citizens, as well as made available in bulk purchases to school cafeterias.

How — A Cure for an Unhealthy Culture

For those who doubt that we can see a cultural change in the health of our nation, I would point out that we have already seen several cultural shifts in our nation in my own lifetime. In the early 1960s, litter on our highways and in our streets was a huge problem. Seatbelts were an aftermarket device rarely selected by motorists and almost never used by drivers or their passengers. Smoking was so prevalent that many doctors had a cigarette in their hand or mouth while extolling the virtues of good health to their patients. Nonsmokers were forced to breathe in the toxic fumes of secondhand smoke in cars, airplanes, restaurants, and meeting rooms. It was considered rude not to provide ashtrays, and even more rude to ask a smoker to put out a cigarette. Drunkenness and even drunk driving was considered fodder for comedy, with comics such as Foster Brooks and celebrities like Dean Martin building their routines around the hilarity of being falling-down drunk.

Today, it is quite unfashionable to litter and most states have steep fines for those caught in the act. In my own state, we installed toll-free telephone lines so people can easily report anyone seen littering in Arkansas. The license plate of the person is researched and a letter is sent indicating the time and place that litter was seen coming out of the vehicle. Three such warning letters can constitute probable cause for a fine.

Seatbelts are not only required as a part of standard features of an automobile but states now require their use and levy fines for those who drive unbuckled.

Smoking disappeared long ago on airplanes. Increasingly, many cities and states have banned any indoor smoking in the workplace, where the deadly secondhand smoke infringes upon the right of another to breathe clean air.

One of my proudest moments as governor was signing the Indoor Clean Air Act in 2006, which virtually eliminates smoking in our state in any workplace with few exceptions or exemptions. Amazingly, some tried to defend blowing their smoke on other people, even claiming it was the "conservative view" because it was a property rights issue. No real conservative would believe that one person has the right to confiscate another person's property without just compensation, cause, or contract. A person should not have his or her health stolen or confiscated by the senseless act of a tobacco user who insists on lighting up and inflicting his or her habit on a person who chooses not to smoke.

As part of my own personal health regimen, I don't eat sugar or sweets, but I don't begrudge others who still enjoy them. If, however, someone took a candy bar, held me down, and shoved it in my mouth, forcing me to ingest it, I would certainly be offended. Somehow, people don't see the similarity when they light up a cigarette—indulging in their own habit as they impose it on others—instead of taking it outdoors. They choose to force others around them to inhale these noxious chemicals that are far more deadly in that form than most people realize.

Mothers Against Drunk Driving (MADD) made it pretty clear that there is nothing funny about an intoxicated person, especially those who get behind the wheel of an automobile and kill innocent people. As a result of their efforts, states have stiffened the penalties for drunk driving and public intoxication, and alcohol treatment centers have sprung up nationally to treat people whose addiction to alcohol is out of control.

In each of these four areas that caused cultural shifts, there are three observable steps to move the needle from one side of the gauge to the other.

First, there were changes in *attitudes*. Through advertising, public awareness campaigns, and education efforts, public sentiment toward litter, seatbelts, smoking, and drunk driving was reshaped. Through Lady Bird Johnson's Keep America Beautiful campaign in the early 1960s and the crash dummies, which vividly showed us what happens in an impact collision without seatbelts, we started seeing the light. We banned the marketing of cigarette products on television and started airing public health commercials releasing medical information about the dangers of tobacco use. We also featured mothers whose children were killed by drunk drivers in commercials, openly challenging the humor of drunkenness.

As attitudes shifted, a second phase began and we observed a change in the *atmosphere* surrounding these issues. "No Litter" signs and trash receptacles in convenient places were an atmospheric reminder that it was wrong to litter and it was right to properly dispose of one's trash. The required presence of seatbelts and subsequent awareness campaigns to "Buckle Up for Safety" moved Americans to do more than sit on their seatbelts when they drove. Removing ashtrays, placing "No Smoking" signs, designating no-smoking areas in restaurants, and creating no-smoking rooms in hotels changed the atmosphere in which smoking was considered acceptable. Designated driver campaigns and free cab rides home after holiday celebrations provided by civic organizations helped change the atmosphere of drinking.

Finally, once attitudes changed and the atmosphere surrounding certain behaviors began to shift, specific *actions* were taken by government that forever changed the culture of these four lifestyles. Fines for littering are prevalent in most states; the use of a seatbelt is no longer merely encouraged but required and enforced; smoking is increasingly prohibited in indoor areas and lighting up and projecting smoke on others is considered a form of truly boorish behavior; and now many states have stiff fines, loss of privileges, and heavy jail or prison time for driving while intoxicated.

There are those who believe that America cannot break or shake its addiction to fried, sugary, and over-salted foods. Those people believe that we are incapable of shifting our unhealthy culture, which is making us fatter, unhealthier, and more likely to die prematurely. History shows that we can, in fact, help Americans to change, not by force-feeding them government restrictions or requirements but by first changing attitudes and the atmosphere in which we live. Eventually, having shifted public opinion, we can solidify the attitude and atmospheric changes with government actions to statutorily define the will of the majority.

* * *

We have aggressively acted in Arkansas to change the culture of health. As I looked at the cost, it became increasingly apparent that the impact of poor health for our state employees, our ever-growing Medicaid population, and to private business was nonsustainable.

In the private sector, major American institutional giants like General Motors face economic ruin in large measure because of the spiraling cost of health care for employees and pensioners. In 2006, GM was spending more money on health benefits for its employees than it spends to purchase steel for its automobiles. Each GM car had built into its price about $1,500 to cover the health care costs of the workers who built it. The purchase of a General Motors vehicle is no longer the purchase of an automobile—the car is given to the consumer as a thank-you for helping fund the care of the employees who are getting increasingly ill with chronic diseases.

Even a young visionary and entrepreneurially avant-garde company like Starbucks is faced with similar challenges. Starbucks works hard to be on the cutting edge of environmental responsibility and corporate generosity, and has been heralded as a model company for providing health care benefits to its employees. It has helped move the marketing of coffee from a home-brewed morning beverage to something along the lines of the quest for the Holy Grail, with people lined up for blocks to purchase the aromatic and favorable brew. But in 2005, Howard Schultz, the CEO of Starbucks, said that he would have to spend more money covering the cost of health care of his employees than purchasing coffee for the entire Starbucks chain!

During my tenure as governor of Arkansas, we launched the Healthy Arkansas initiative, which was later expanded to the Healthy America initiative during my chairmanship of the National Governors Association. The focus was on helping change the culture of health, in part by providing incentives for people to make personal lifestyle changes that would result in healthier behaviors, more satisfactory outcomes, and lower costs.

We provide insurance discounts for those who agree not to smoke and who will do a health risk assessment each year. The combined savings can be as much as $480 per year, which for a state employee can be a nice incentive. We started providing 1-800 numbers for people to access health coaches for information on everything from disease management to blood pressure checks, to nutritional tips, to coaching assistance for smoking cessation. We became the first state in the nation to offer smoking cessation toolkits that include nicotine patches, counseling, and other assistance to both state employees and those of the Medicaid population to get them off the nicotine addiction. We eliminated copays and deductibles for screenings required for mammography, colonoscopy, and prostate cancer exams. For many, the copays and deductibles were a financial impediment, but the screenings mean early detection, much less expensive treatment, and saved lives. The Central Arkansas Veterans Health Care System found that for every dollar spent in a health or wellness program, they saved eight dollars in health care costs.

It never has made sense to me that an insurance plan would pay $300,000 to $400,000 for the cost of a quadruple bypass and the rehabilitation from open heart surgery, but would not cover a $75 session with a nutrition counselor to learn how to eat healthier foods and perhaps avoid the heart attack altogether. We began to give employees walk breaks during office hours, realizing that if smokers were given the regular opportunities during the workday to slowly kill themselves smoking, it surely made sense to give employees a few minutes a day to go for a vigorous walk. Those who took a walk would be not only healthier but more alert while at their desk or workstation. We developed a Web site filled not only with useful health tips but listing county-specific information on the location of walking and hiking trails and resources within specific local communities. We partnered with Gerber and Wal-Mart to publish and distribute hundreds of thousands of pocket-size health guidebooks aimed at families who struggle with ways to improve nutrition, exercise, and healthy habits. We also started covering medically supervised weight loss programs under the state employees' health plan.

States all over the country have been engaging in innovative and creative ways to help save money for the taxpayers and save the lives of citizens. While Washington seems incapable of moving toward any reforms in health care, states have been on the forefront of innovative ideas. If necessity is the mother of invention, then the necessity of making more prudent decisions in the expenditure of health care dollars has created sanity for states that our federal government has lacked the will to demonstrate. Unlike the federal government, which can merely print more money or pass the cost onto states, governors are required to balance budgets, solve problems, and don't have the luxury of borrowing against the future. In many cases we are discovering that it is not a radical, revolutionary shift that must occur but acceptable, gradual, and manageable steps that add up to real differences.

America on the Move, an organization that encourages people to become physically active, is a perfect example. They don't force people to sign up for two-hour-a-day sweat sessions with a professional trainer, but rather encourage simple adjustments in daily routines such as taking the stairs instead of elevators, walking from the far end of the parking lot instead of next to the door, and making modest changes in food consumption. America on the Move points out that reducing your total caloric intake by 100 calories a day results in a ten-pound-a-year weight loss.

It is equally alarming that while absenteeism due to chronic disease plagues our nation, another health risk challenges our productivity with what Ronald Kessler of Harvard Medical School calls "presenteeism." An employee may be physically present at work, but due to the effects of chronic health problems, has a 60 percent loss of productivity. At a time in our nation's life when we are in a challenging state of competition with emerging nations such as China and India, we can ill afford to have significant numbers of our workforce physically present at a workstation but essentially incapable of carrying out the job.

In fact, other steps could be taken that would not only result in significant savings and better health but provide the all-elusive access to affordable health care coverage for every American. According to a study by the RAND Corporation, the impact of errors associated with antiquated paper medical records cost an unnecessary $160 million a year. Electronic medical records would not only be more efficient but would be far better for the patients in providing a greater level of accuracy, not to mention the portability of personal health records.

In 1988, Derrick Redman of the United Kingdom was scheduled to run the 400-meter event in the Seoul Summer Olympics. Ten minutes before the race for which he had trained a lifetime, he had to withdraw due to an injury in his Achilles tendon. One can only imagine the disappointment and devastation of having prepared for years only to have to withdraw from competition moments before the event. Five surgeries later, and after extensive rehabilitation efforts on his part, Derrick Redman was ready to try again at the Summer Olympics in Barcelona in 1992. He got off to a good start and appeared to be on his way for an excellent finish. But in the final turn he ruptured a hamstring, collapsing to the track in pain. The physical pain was perhaps made insignificant by the deep emotional pain of having come so far and overcome so much, only to have it end one turn shy of the finish line. Derrick Redman's father, who had watched his son spend his life training and preparing and who had been with him through most of his competitions, watched in horror from the stands as his son's body crumpled on the track below. Instinctively, he leapt from his seat, brushed past security guards, ran onto the track, and scooped his son up in his arms. Both Derrick and his father were weeping, but his father helped him to his feet, put Derrick's arm around his shoulder so that he could limp his way for the final steps, and said, "We will just finish this one together."

As a father of three grown children, I can only imagine the agony Derrick Redman's father felt. While the crushing blow to Derrick of being unable to finish would hurt beyond words, every father can understand that there is no greater pain than to see the suffering of one's offspring. It will be a great tragedy if today's American fathers—and mothers—have to watch helplessly as their children's generation collapses on the track and cannot finish because of unhealthy habits.

We are a nation that historically has made course corrections when needed. We have been able to change our culture time and time again. It doesn't just happen. It requires leadership and vision and tenacity, not only among our leaders but within the imagination of our people, to make it happen. I hope that every father and every mother in America will join me in believing that the battle to make America a healthy nation is a battle worth fighting. We all must commit to personally engage in being part of perhaps the most challenging, but important, shift in the history of our country.

12 Action Steps to STOP
the Culture of Chronic Disease

1. Don't smoke—PERIOD!

2. Exercise a minimum of three times per week, at least thirty minutes per session.

3. Set specific, challenging, but realistic fitness goals for the month and the year.

4. Eliminate processed sugar from your diet as much as possible, if not totally.

5. Don't eat anything with partially hydrogenated vegetable oil (trans fat).

6. Eat five servings a day minimum of fruits and vegetables.

7. Insist on only whole grain breads, pastas, and cereals.

8. Eliminate fried foods from your diet.

9. Look for ways to become an empowered health consumer.

10. Regularly read articles and books on health and fitness.

11. Do little things like taking the stairs instead of elevators, parking in the far end of parking lots, and walking to do errands.

12. Sleep more!

Chapter 5

STOP ABUSING OUR PLANET

You don't have to hug a tree to appreciate one. It would have been a mistake to sign the Kyoto Treaty since it would have given foreign nations the power to impose standards on us they wouldn't impose on themselves. And Al Gore wasn't entirely wrong when he spoke of earth "in the balance." Balance is exactly what we need more of in an honest discussion about the environment. All of us need to have a healthy respect for our resources, a responsible level of use of those resources, and a comprehensive plan for either preserving or renewing those resources.

In June 1996 we were in the transition period between the late May resignation of Governor Jim Guy Tucker and my swearing in, which was scheduled for July 15. I had been asked to have lunch at the Stephens Building in downtown Little Rock with Game and Fish Commissioner Witt Stephens Jr., Richard Davies, director of the Arkansas Department of Parks and Tourism, and Steve Wilson, director of the Arkansas Game and Fish Commission. The purpose of the lunch was to discuss a proposed state constitutional amendment that was set for the ballot in November 1996, placed there by the Arkansas legislature. If enacted by the people, this amendment would dedicate one eighth of a cent in sales tax to the conservation of the natural resources of our state. Forty-five percent of the proceeds would go to Parks and Tourism, 45 percent to the

Game and Fish Commission, 9 percent to the Department of Arkansas Heritage, and 1 percent to the Keep Arkansas Beautiful Commission.

Arkansas's moniker is "the Natural State." For outdoor enthusiasts it is perhaps the best-kept secret in all of North America. It has 9,700 miles of navigable streams, over 650 thousand acres of lakes, and hundreds of thousands of acres of forest land with every kind of topography imaginable from majestic scenic mountains to lush forest and some of the most extensive marsh and prairie land in the nation.

Arkansas is renowned as a paradise for those who enjoy hunting, fishing, canoeing, hiking, or bird-watching. It has long been known as the duck hunting capital of the world because of its strategic location along the Mississippi flyway and due to the small town of Stuttgart, Arkansas, home of the World Championship Duck Calling Contest.

Arkansas is home to several world records in fishing, including the largest walleye, brown trout, and striper. It is the manufacturing home of renowned boat builders such as Ranger, Bass Cat, War Eagle, and Express, and hosts some of the premier fly-fishing on streams such as the White, Norfolk, Little Red, and Little Missouri Rivers. Over 22 million visitors come to Arkansas each year, many engaging in some form of outdoor adventure for at least part of their visit.

The ballot measure slated for November of that year was a crucial one for Arkansas's future. During the previous twenty years, four attempts had been made to place a similar measure before the people and they had either been tied up in court battles and failed to make the ballot or had been defeated due to concerns expressed by opponents over issues ranging from cost to control.

My position as a conservative Republican with a disdain for excessive taxation is well earned. As lieutenant governor I had successfully led an effort to defeat a massive tax proposal to fund a road-building program. The state certainly needed a road program in the most desperate of ways, but this particular proposal had an especially high price with a variety of tax sources. Even worse, it would have funded some of the least traveled roads in the state, doing nothing to repair our crumbling interstate highways, which were ranked among the worst in the nation.

My hosts for the luncheon were polite, but obviously apprehensive about discussing the ballot initiative, which would have dedicated tax monies to conservation. They gently and gingerly explained the need for a dedicated funding stream to preserve the natural resources of the state. At one point Witt Stephens Jr. made his appeal and said, "Governor, we hope that you will not actively campaign against the measure."

I smiled and replied, "Gentleman, I can assure you I won't be campaigning *against* the proposal, and in fact I am strongly in favor of it!"

A stunned silence filled the room as they looked at one another and then back to me. I still can recall Richard Davies's puzzled look as he asked, "Did you say you are *for* the amendment?"

"Not only am I for it but I would like to know if it would be helpful if I actively campaigned for its passage in the fall," I replied.

There has been a perception that conservative Republicans don't care much for the environment or the protection and preservation of natural resources. I remind people that the very word "conservative" means that we are all about conserving those things that are valuable and dear. Few things are more valuable to us than the natural resources that God created and gave to us to responsibly and carefully manage so as to pass them on to the next generation in as good, if not better, shape than we found them.

One of the proudest moments I have had as a governor is the passage of what became Amendment 75 to the Arkansas Constitution. It forever dedicates a small but vital revenue stream to the conservation of our state's vast, valuable, and irreplaceable resources.

Prior to being unexpectedly thrust into the governor's office, I was engaged in a candidacy for the United States Senate, which I abandoned in order to finish out the term as governor of my predecessor. As part of what would have been my Senate campaign in 1996, I had already planned to tour the entire length of the Arkansas River, from the Oklahoma border to the Mississippi River where the Arkansas River empties. It was my intention to make the entire trip of 308 miles in my boat, a sleek twenty-one-foot Bass Cat equipped with a high-horsepower Mercury Outboard OptiMax capable of skimming the water at speeds exceeding seventy miles an hour. The idea for this trip wasn't speed, however, but a series of stops for campaign rallies. We would do it from water's edge as a unique way of highlighting the extraordinary and unparalleled beauty only viewable along the Arkansas River. Some of the views by way of the river were unlike any that could be seen by road, rail, or air.

That October 1996 trip will remain one of my most memorable experiences as governor. My wife joined me for the entire distance on a personal watercraft, earning her the nickname "Jet-ski Janet." We were accompanied by a flotilla of boats, including party barges packed with press, and other crafts carrying supplies for the week-long effort, which took us diagonally across the entire breadth of Arkansas, from the northwest to the southeast. Most observers credit the trip—with its very high media visibility and the advocacy that was created across the state—as crucial to the passage of the amendment.

A major part of my motivation for being so strongly in favor of this effort was a deeply held conviction that we have a responsibility to treat our natural resources as a *treasure* and not as *trash*. Some of this is rooted in my childhood days as a Boy Scout, when it was drilled into me to always leave a campsite and the woods in as good a condition as I found them.

A much deeper part of that conviction comes from my own personal faith, which reminds me that "the earth is the Lord's" and that we are not its owners; merely its caretakers. From the very first pages of Genesis in the Old Testament we are reminded that God is the Creator and we are responsible for tending to that which he created; to preserve it and to protect it. We are indeed given the liberty and in fact the admonition to enjoy and to utilize the resources, but *use* is not *abuse* and we have no right to pillage the planet unmercifully. We should see to it that our care for the environment enhances not only its aesthetic value but preserves the resources themselves for future generations.

The passage of this amendment was also important to me because I recognized that for many people in my state, the enjoyment of the woods and water was a part of our culture and especially vital to the quality of life enjoyed by all people regardless of their socioeconomic status. As a child growing up barely above the poverty line, it was assumed that even a poor kid could go fishing or hunting or hiking or camping. While our families might not have the financial resources to go to Disneyland or visit a beach, we would be able to access public lakes for fishing or swimming or picnicking, and parks would freely give every child the opportunity to enjoy the great treasures of the outdoors.

It is often said that "every child in Arkansas is within a bike ride of a fishing hole," and one of the passions that I have had is to ensure that hunting, fishing, and other outdoor experiences were not limited to the affluent who could afford memberships in expensive hunting or fishing clubs, but rather accessible to all our citizens. It's especially important to the father or mother who works hard all week and hopes to be able to have a few moments with their children on the weekend enjoying the outdoors.

In the ten years following the passage of Amendment 75, Arkansas has been able to obtain and set aside over 31,000 acres to be enjoyed by all citizens. Some of the state's premier hunting lands were kept from being gobbled up by out-of-state private investors who would have made those treasured acres off-limits to kids who grew up like me. I knew that had it not been for publicly accessible land, I would never have grown up loving the outdoors and enjoying fishing and later hunting.

I am unapologetically a conservationist and believe that one of America's urgent crises is taking better care of our magnificent homeland and all its rich and varied beauty "from sea to shining sea." I do, however, see a distinction between being a "conservationist" and "environmentalist." A conservationist cares deeply about the environment and wishes to act as a responsible steward of it, yet recognizes that we may appropriately use renewable resources to sustain life. Environmentalists often feel that we are to have an almost equal respect and reverence for the created as for the Creator. We should worship the Creator, but respect and take care of that which is *created*.

Those of us whose pleasures and passions are found in our love of the outdoors appreciate the value of clean air, clean water, and good soil as much as—and in a much more practical way than—those who claim to love the environment but actually spend very little time outside of their own personal concrete and steel jungles of urban life.

Arkansas added 150,000 acres of new forests during my tenure as governor, debunking the notion that harvesting trees is depleting forests. I know that without careful management of our forest and the periodic harvesting of wood, the brush and timber becomes so thick so as to overwhelm the nutrients in the soil and water that helps the trees grow. Failing to harvest any trees can create an environment for timber-consuming insects and, even worse, wildfires that can destroy in hours what took hundreds of years to grow. I can also appreciate the fact that carefully regulated hunting ensures that herds of various species do not overpopulate, making it difficult for there to be an adequate food supply, and eventually leading to the endangerment if not extinction of certain species. Nonhunters think those who stalk and take wild game threaten the existence of the wildlife, when in fact it is the license fees of the hunters that pay for food plots and habitat, and the management of the game, ensuring its continuation.

Many of us who are particularly fond of duck hunting, turkey hunting, and fishing contribute time and resources to conservation organizations such as Ducks Unlimited, Delta Waterfowl, the National Wild Turkey Federation, and other organizations that pour millions of dollars into the care, feeding, and preservation of the species. I am personally a life member of Ducks Unlimited as well as a life member of Bassmasters.

Belonging to these organizations not only provides me with information but enables me to invest for the long-term future enjoyment of these great American traditions. I am also a longtime member of the National Rifle Association, which is an effective voice for the preservation of Second Amendment rights to firearms ownership for sporting as well as personal protection.

I must confess that I have been guilty in the past of overheated rhetoric related to some whose extreme environmentalism seemed to lose a sense of perspective and balance. I once made a speech widely reported by the press in which I referred with disdain to a group of environmentalists. In the midst of wildfires in California, they protested property owners using bulldozers to dig trenches and protect their homes from the destruction from the wildfire, fearing that it would imperil the habitat of a certain species of rodent. I called those people "environmental wackos," and while I still believe human life should take priority over that of a rodent, I realize that my choice of terms had done less to encourage meaningful dialogue and more to simply stir up the passions of those who already agreed with me.

An encouraging sign in the past few years is that many conservative

Christian leaders are also joining in the call for us to take a much more active role in caring for the environment as well as conserving energy. I am ashamed to say that for the most part, people of faith have been far too silent on this issue, especially in light of the unmistakable biblical mandate to take care of the earth and to recognize that the abuse of our planet is a sin against the God who created it, and who expects us to care for it.

Land development and the natural growth of communities can be a good thing, but it also must be balanced with thoughtful thorough planning so as to not disrupt the ecosystem, including vital areas of wetlands, which serve as a natural filter for our resources.

While I understand that building dams on streams can sometimes be useful in flood control, the creation of water reservoirs necessary for sustaining life, or for the production of electricity, we must be careful to balance our use of those resources to ensure that we do not lose all our natural treasures by altering them.

In the 1960s and early 1970s conservationists in Arkansas successfully fought back attempts to build a dam on the Buffalo River in North Arkansas, the phenomenal stream that became America's first National River. To this day it is one of the most magnificently beautiful and vibrant natural streams on the continent. Every time I experience a canoe float down the Buffalo I realize I owe an extraordinary amount of gratitude to some stubborn conservationist from a previous generation who kept the Buffalo River from becoming little more than a memory for old-timers to talk about.

We further abuse the planet by our reckless consumption of energy in all its forms and our growing dependence on foreign sources for our energy needs. The potential economic calamity that this dependence could lead to is real. We have been periodically confronted with crises in our energy supply during the past thirty-five years, but have yet to take seriously our careless energy consumption and lack of production.

Our bodies sometimes send us a signal that something is wrong, and prompt us to call our doctors or even head to the emergency room. Pain is our friend when it leads us to a diagnosis of a deep-seated physical ailment that could imperil our health or our very lives. When we ignore pain or simply mask it with analgesics, we might temporarily feel better but could be lulled into believing that we are healthy when in fact we are merely anesthetized. Our national "policies" of dealing with high energy prices, such as giving people a temporary tax break or suspending the gasoline tax for a brief period of time, is like taking aspirin to cover an underlying disease.

I was in college in 1973 when the oil embargo and sudden spike in gasoline prices caused motorists to experience long lines at gas pumps and prompted a federal mandate of lowering the speed limit to fifty-five miles per hour as a conservation measure. During the past thirty-five years we have chronically experienced an increased demand, a shortened supply, sudden steep and shocking price spikes, and renewed chatter about our need for a new energy policy. Unfortunately, nothing ever comes of it and before long the "crisis" diminishes, and prices get lower (but usually never to the level they were before). We are lulled into thinking all is well.

America increasingly relies on foreign (and sometimes hostile foreign) sources for our fossil fuel demands, creating a cancerous energy policy. Instead of aggressively attempting to remove the cancer and restore our health from within, we are addicted to painkillers to help treat what President Bush called "our addiction to foreign oil."

In November 1973, President Richard Nixon responded to OPEC's oil embargo against us by establishing Project Independence, which promised energy independence by 1980. President Gerald Ford pushed it to 1985, and President Jimmy Carter, who encouraged us to wear sweaters and turn down the thermostat, extended it to 1990, and so has it gone. Whether Democrats or Republicans, presidents or Congress, we claim to be serious about changing our energy dependency but do nothing to make it true.

The volatility of our supplies coming from Iraq, Iran, Nigeria, or Venezuela is only part of the problem we face with our dependence on foreign oil. An equal or greater threat is the demand from rapidly emerging nations, in particular India or China, which means whatever the production, the marketplace will be demanding yet more and more. According to the National Resources Defense Council, Americans spend more than

$200,000 per minute on foreign oil, some $13 million per hour. More than $25 billion a year goes for Persian Gulf imports alone. At the current rate the United States is projected to consume more than 28 million barrels of oil a day by the year 2025—44 percent more oil than we use today. And yet, the United States will not be the only nation gobbling up more of these limited resources. During the next twenty-five years, consumption of industrializing nations will double from 15 to 32 million barrels of oil a day. To meet that need, global oil output would have to expand by more than 50 percent between the years 2005 and 2025.

It is time for the United States to stop its periodic gimmicks and continued reliance on oil primarily produced beyond our borders and by nations who are not exactly America's best friends. Even those who do act more cordially toward us are not producing oil with a benevolent spirit but are driven by their own interests. From December 2003 through 2005, OPEC nations spent more than $13 million lobbying the federal government, and $6.6 million of that came from Saudi Arabia alone! We all should be somewhat discomforted by the amount of money that our policymakers are having tossed their way to keep the addiction alive. It's like passing out glasses of wine at a meeting of Alcoholics Anonymous.

Even as we *increase* our *consumption* of energy, we dramatically *limit* our *production*, making us even more vulnerable to outside sources to fuel our cars and our economy. We have not built a new refinery in thirty years. Politics has kept us from developing potential exploration in the Arctic National Wildlife Refuge, or along the Outer Continental Shelf, and the lack of leadership toward alternative forms of energy has left us with little more than higher prices and a growing anxiety.

It is one thing when the fuel on a private Gulfstream jet means that a very wealthy person has to limit his weekend trip to the Florida coast instead of Europe. The greater challenge is for families operating on a marginal income who find it impossible to heat their homes and fill their tanks with enough gas just to get to and from work.

No longer should this debate be between Democrats and Republicans because both sides have miserably failed to ignite what must happen in order to achieve energy independence, namely the national will to survive. Americans must be convinced that our growing dependence on external sources for fuel and dramatically rising costs threaten our economy and our very existence.

I know that when my own medical doctor sat me down and told me that my lifestyle would kill me in a decade, then and only then did my desire to regain my health become such an obsession that I started viewing a plate of fried chicken with biscuits and gravy not as a temptation but rather as my mortal enemy. It is time we start seeing those barrels of imported oil not as a mere temptation but as our mortal enemy. Those barrels represent the lifeblood of repressive regimes and terrorists as much as they do our indulgence.

This nation has a history of rising to the occasion when it has to. From digging out of the Depression, or mobilizing during World War II, or our quest to be the first nation to put a man on the moon and return him home safely, we have the capacity to use willpower and creativity and do things differently. It's time that we realize the absolute necessity of ending our economic dependence on oil!

One energy source that makes perfect sense for America to aggressively explore and dramatically increase is the production and use of biofuels. The most common biofuels are ethanol and biodiesel, both of which have the potential of decreasing our dependence on oil, but could also have a dramatic and positive impact on America's agricultural production. It could give our farmers the ability to feed and fuel us. While the cost of converting a biofuel source to usable fuel has been historically expensive and therefore not as attractive as gasoline, creating incentives with potential hefty financial rewards could be valuable in the production of ethanol and biodiesel. New technologies using forms of biomass are increasingly viable, and the production of these would be controlled within our own borders. An added advantage of biofuels is that unlike gasoline and conventional diesel, they contain oxygen, which allows petroleum products to burn more completely, reducing air pollution and cutting back on the buildup of greenhouse gases.

Other alternative energy sources such as solar or wind have great potential in that they occur naturally, are therefore environmentally friendly, and have an inexhaustible source. There are certainly limitations, particularly to sources such as wind energy because of the intermittent nature of wind power. Some have suggested building a turbine next to the United States Capitol, since quite a bit of "wind" has blown from the building in speeches and it has yet to be captured for much that is meaningful!

Hydrogen cells or other types of fuel cells also have potential, but are not yet fully developed in a cost-efficient manner to make them practical on a wide-scale basis. Fuel cells still have tremendous promise, however, in that they do not produce air pollutants that create smog and cause health problems. When pure hydrogen is used as a fuel, fuel cells emit only heat and water as a by-product.

While many Americans still fear nuclear power, we would be wise to explore ways to harness it for purposes more peaceful and productive than the building of bombs. The growing anxiety and restlessness over the impact of suddenly spiking gasoline, natural gas, and electricity costs have created near panic in the homes of many Americans. Many small business owners are threatened out of existence because of the escalating costs from uncontrollable energy expenses. People who are impoverished and on the brink of financial disaster can be pushed over the edge when they simply don't have the money to pay their electric bill and can't afford to pay for transportation to make it to work.

These concerns cannot be adequately met by merely changing the source of fuel or addressing the consumption of petroleum, but must include the willingness of Americans to engage in serious conservation efforts to manage their consumption.

12 Action Steps to STOP Abusing Our Planet

1. Never litter!

2. Report littering if your state has a litter hotline; if not, advocate for one.

3. Conserve gas by combining trips to do errands—better yet, walk or ride a bike.

4. Carpool to work or school.

5. Walk or bike whenever you can.

6. Turn off lights and appliances when not in use.

7. Have an energy audit of your home.

8. Spend time outdoors hiking, bird-watching, hunting, or fishing.

9. Keep your car maintained and serviced for better fuel efficiency.

10. Take your family camping.

11. Recycle paper, glass, plastic, and cans.

12. Learn more about renewable fuel sources and consider energy-efficient appliances and construction processes (for example, geothermal).

Chapter 6

STOP THE REVENGE-BASED CRIMINAL JUSTICE SYSTEM

Bobby Ray Fretwell was days away from a February 16, 1999, execution that I had set some forty-five days earlier. With a stroke of a pen, my signature had set in motion a process that was to bring closure to a crime that he had committed years before in Marshall, Arkansas, the county seat of Searcy County and one of the most remote and rural areas of the Ozark Mountains. Fretwell had exhausted his appeals and had already been moved from death row to a special holding cell at Cummins prison, where he would await the final days prior to his scheduled execution.

Part of the rationale for moving a condemned person to a different facility just prior to execution is that those who have worked with and guarded the prisoner for years of incarceration on death row will not have to be the ones to actually carry out the execution. The death penalty is difficult enough on total strangers, but is especially emotional for those who have dealt with the inmate through the more mellow years.

As has been the case in every one of the death penalty cases that I have dealt with as governor, I reviewed every single page of every single document available, including court transcripts of the trial, appeals, and documents of evidence such as crime scene and autopsy photographs.

Some of those images from death penalty cases are indelibly etched on my mind and haunt me to this day.

The death penalty is the only decision that I make as a governor that is totally irrevocable. There is no "do-over." Once an execution is carried out, a life has ended. Executions are the law's most drastic measure against a person who has committed a crime so heinous that a jury concluded the only appropriate response would be that the guilty person's life be forfeited in return for the innocent life taken.

As has been my practice, I kept the large box of file folders with the case documents near my desk to review them a second time in the days prior to the execution. One particularly troubling and unsettling part of the evidence was a videotape of interviews conducted with Fretwell and his brother. The description of their early family life was gut-wrenching and revealed a childhood of abuse, humiliation, and degradation at the hands of a violent father. I was moved to tears by the revolting manner in which these men had been raised, but that did not alter the circumstances of the crime he had committed.

Fretwell had committed the especially brutal and meaningless murder of Sherman Sullins, an elderly and decent gentleman who, like so many people of Searcy County, was as God-fearing, hardworking, and honest as a man could be. He had raised a family who also had followed his steps of hard work and honesty. While not a family of great wealth, they were indeed the kind of people who were well respected and appreciated for treating others with kindness. They paid bills on time and gave people their money's worth for work they performed. Perhaps their greatest wealth was the close-knit bond that spanned at least three living generations.

Fretwell's murder of this kind of gentleman—committed to get Mr. Sullins's money—was exacerbated by the fact that the killing was done in the man's own home. To add insult to injury, after the savage killing, Fretwell took the man's truck for his escape. His wife came home and found her husband's lifeless body. For such a brutal and senseless crime, Fretwell deserved the death penalty as much as anyone who had been sentenced to it.

No matter what unforgivable circumstances affected his childhood, nothing could excuse or justify his actions. After careful review of his case, I concluded that the system had functioned properly and would complete its course the moment Bobby Fretwell paid the ultimate price for the ultimate crime.

But something then happened that would change Bobby Fretwell's life—and mine—forever.

A few days before the scheduled execution, a conscientious young attorney who oversaw criminal justice cases in my office came to me with some startling news. A person who had been on the jury in Fretwell's case had come forward and revealed he had been told that if Fretwell was found guilty, he would get life in prison without possibility of parole, not the death sentence. This juror, realizing that Fretwell was about to be executed, felt compelled to speak up. He had been promised that the death penalty would not be carried out. That was the reason he had voted for a guilty verdict.

If true, this would be not only a shocking piece of new evidence but certainly would alter the basis on which the state was about to take a man's life. According to the juror, the public defender assigned to the Fretwell case gave less than a stellar performance, which was confirmed by the court transcript.

For me, I felt there was no choice but to order a stay of execution until the facts could be sorted out. Frankly, I could have easily ignored what had been presented to me and attributed it to an unnecessary and unfounded remorse on the part of a juror. Fretwell was a lifelong reprobate who had no real family or friends whose lives would be dramatically affected by his execution. I could ignore what had been presented to me and go forward with the execution. Politically, it was the safest decision to make. But I couldn't and wouldn't do that.

The problem I faced was that I was unable and unwilling to spend the rest of my life looking each day in the mirror at a man who had ignored late evidence in a death penalty case in order to avoid the complications that come with clemency. It was simply not an option. If the justice system would not work for the "least of these among us," then neither would it work for me or anyone else.

After issuing a stay of execution in order to more thoroughly check out the juror's story, additional information surfaced that made his sentence even more troubling. The process in Arkansas states that for a governor to issue a clemency, he must first make public such an intention and allow a period of thirty days for public comment to be received. I announced my intentions to commute Bobby Ray Fretwell's death sentence to one of life in prison without parole, and waited for what I knew would be a very strong reaction.

The wait was not long.

The family and an overwhelming number of people in Searcy County were outraged, and understandably so. The jurors begged for anonymity for fear that their lives and reputations in the small community would be severely damaged. People would feel their coming forward kept their neighbor's murderer alive for yet another day. The news was especially difficult for the family of the gentleman murdered by Fretwell. The family asked to visit with me to discuss the case and their strong feelings. I knew such a meeting would be emotional and painful, but also felt that this dear family deserved no less. A meeting was scheduled. Protesters held a vigil at the gates of the Governor's Mansion and angry letters and phone calls poured into my office. At the designated time, I hosted the Sullinses in an emotional two-hour meeting. They showed me the photos of their husband, father, and grandfather while he was alive, and of the same man at the crime scene.

There was nothing I could say or do to bring comfort. I could not blame this family for their anger and felt had the circumstances been reversed, I would have been equally upset as they rightfully were. As much as I wanted to accommodate their desire to bring closure to this long nightmare by carrying out the execution as planned, I knew that to do so would be a violation of the very oath I took as governor. More important, I had a responsibility to God to treat all people, even Bobby Ray Fretwell, as I would treat the Lord himself. To this day, the pain of that day still grieves me; the depth of their sorrow and their rightful sense of outrage could not be calmed by word or action.

It was a stark and solemn reminder to me that our justice system is far from perfect, and the pain of a victim cannot be overcome with any level of sentence or amount of money in restitution. We are vividly reminded that on this side of the grave some things are simply not fair and the ledger will never be even or made right. But the criminal justice system of America is unique, and while it recognizes imperfection, it follows the premise that justice should be blind and should be equal.

Whether we should even have a death penalty is a tough issue. I believe some crimes deserve it, but that does *not* mean that I like it. While I do believe it should be an option, my attitude has never been like those who boast of how they'd "gladly pull the switch." Carrying out the death penalty was unquestionably the worst part of my job as governor. Seventeen times I sat by a phone with a line open to the death chamber for the two hours before the scheduled moment and waited for either a court-ordered reprieve or the report from the correction director that the procedure was ready to be carried out. I then gave the verbal order that fulfilled what my signature had initiated approximately forty-five days earlier. Once the order was given, a lethal injection was administered and we waited from four to fifteen minutes until the condemned man or woman was pronounced dead. I never slept well those nights. I did the job that the law prescribed for me to do, but I hated every minute of it. I always felt that it was not only an execution of a person who committed a terrible murder; it was a reminder that through years of trials and appeals, no alternative was determined to be more appropriate than to end a human life.

Some wonder how a person so pro-life as me could accept the law of a death penalty. But a death sentence is a result of a lengthy and thorough judicial process applied to a person deemed guilty beyond a reasonable doubt. That's far different from one person singularly deciding to end the life of a totally innocent and helpless unborn child. In that case, there is no process of justice, no evidence of guilt presented, no defense for the condemned child, and no appeal.

It's sometimes been said that the five most feared words for a politician are "Will the defendant please rise." While it is understandable to be afraid of having the criminal justice system used against you, an even greater fear is that those of us who must administer it might do so in a way as to unfairly punish the innocent or fail to properly consequence the guilty. In my earliest memories of reciting the Pledge of Allegiance I was taught that our pledge ended with four words that set our nation apart . . . "and justice for all."

A unique element of our criminal justice system is that it presumes innocence until guilt is proven beyond a reasonable doubt. This very high and, at times, almost unreasonable standard can be frustrating to those who want justice carried out swiftly and harshly. But it is also the basis that gives our society strength and makes us the envy of people the world over.

The hallmark of our system is that its primary function is to protect the innocent of society by removing from our midst those whose inability to play by the rules threatens our peace, property, or personhood. Our system is based on the notion that the ultimate purpose of the criminal justice system—beyond establishing guilt and responsibility—is not to seek mere punishment but to correct the behavior that led to the crime.

America went through a period of permissiveness in the 1970s. In some cases there were those who advocated that criminals really were not bad people, but just individuals who were themselves victims of either poverty or lack of education. They had not learned social skills that the rest of us took for granted. Those who believed in such a view typically favored counseling over incarceration, but rising crime rates and a demand of the public made it clear that "coddling criminals" is a terribly failed idea.

In the 1990s, the pendulum swung harshly back in the opposite direction and very popular policies such as the "three strikes and you're out" and "no parole provision" were adopted. The growth of victims' rights also became a significant part of sentencing laws, and many states adopted new procedures that allowed victims of crime to have not only a more active voice in the adjudication process but often a substantial role in determining the outcome of the proceedings.

Being tough on crime is certainly more popular than being soft, but America needs to be careful that in our attempt to stoutly enforce our laws and protect our citizens, we do not end up with a system that is based more on revenge than restoration.

A revenge-based criminal justice system is one that goes beyond wanting to protect the innocent and holding the guilty accountable for their actions, but seeks to measure out as harsh a judgment as is possible so as to satisfy the natural inclination to get even. There are three aspects we will examine that relate to achieving "justice for all."

The Crisis

In 2006 there were almost 7 million people in prison, on probation, or on parole in the United States, up from 3.2 million in 1990. This represents one in every thirty-one adults in the United States. No nation on earth incarcerates as many people as we do. In fact, we incarcerate far more people than more populated and, it is assumed, more punitive nations such as China, Russia, Brazil, and India. We incarcerate ten times as many people as most other democracies, 726 people per 100,000, and there are six times as many Americans in prison as there are in all of Europe.

Even more troubling is the rate at which young African-American men enter the prison system. As many African-American males have served in prison as have all whites both male and female, despite the significant population disparities between whites and blacks. While disproportionate crime rates are a factor, it is inescapable that an impoverished minority male is less likely to have exceptional defense counsel and more likely to go to prison and do years of hard time. An affluent white male is more likely to get probation and pay a fine.

People who have committed violent crimes and who are likely to do it again most certainly should be locked up in prison for our sake and theirs, but as Larry Norris, the director of the Arkansas Department of Corrections during my tenure, often said, "We lock up a lot of people that we are mad at rather than just the ones we are really afraid of."

The incarceration rate has tripled since 1980, and the average cost to keep someone in prison in the United States is $22,000 a year, whether the person is there for murder or shoplifting. I am not advocating wide-scale release, but rather a rethinking of the purpose of our prisons, making sure that we can afford to pay for the policies that are popular. For the cost of prison we could send someone to any public university in my state and pay full tuition, room, board, books, and have some spending money.

When I became governor in the summer of 1996, there were fewer than eight thousand inmates in the Arkansas prison system. By the time I left office ten and a half years later that number had swelled to nearly 14,000. Approximately 57 percent of those were nonviolent offenders.

One prison official told me that 80 percent of all those incarcerated were there because of drugs or alcohol and that they were either drunk or high when they committed the crime, or they committed the crime in order to get drunk or high. As he astutely observed, we don't have a crime problem, we have a drug and alcohol problem.

While those who deal drugs and entice others into enslaving addictions deserve prison sentences, we end up locking away many nonviolent drug users, some of whom spend longer periods in prison than they would if they had committed a violent crime.

A major reform in dealing with drug offenders in Arkansas was the establishment of drug courts, where a nonviolent drug offender could be directed to enroll in drug treatment programs and heavily supervised community service. Naturally, any violation of good behavior during this period would result in prison, but if the individual successfully completed drug rehabilitation and demonstrated a different behavior, the person's record would be expunged. In Arkansas, the recidivism rate dropped to 31 percent. More significantly, the cost per day was lower than that of prison, and the time expended significantly less, resulting in an overall savings to the taxpayer, while at the same time allowing the offender to regain his or her life.

On June 1, 2006, I attended a dedication service of a faith-based unit in our prison system operated in partnership with InnerChange Freedom Initiative, a division of Prison Fellowship, founded by Charles Colson. It was a culmination of almost five years of effort that brought progress to our system. The intense and demanding program requires eleven months of participation while in prison and an additional twelve months after prison as the inmate reenters society. Recidivism rates for those in the program are 60 percent less than normal. It's bad enough people go to prison the first time; that affirms the personal failure of the criminal. It's worse when that person comes back again, for that affirms both the failure of the criminal and a "corrections" system that failed to "correct."

Another significant change in our approach was a ramping up of community corrections wherein those charged with nonviolent crimes could be sentenced to community service with monitoring and regular reporting to supervisors. The cost per day in the community corrections system is about $7.50 per inmate per day versus the $44.50 per day cost of incarceration. In addition, the offender is employed and actually paying taxes on income earned rather than taking taxpayer money for his or her room and board.

Yet another alternative is the construction of a facility to house "technical violators." Technical violators are those who have been in the system, but either failed to make restitution, report on time to a parole officer, or are guilty of some other type of technical error rather than actually committing a crime. Having a facility dedicated solely to technical violators made it possible to engage those individuals in more community service, less security since they were rarely a risk, and subsequently lower costs, while not being housed with more hardened criminals.

A popular, but ill-conceived notion is the complete elimination of parole or accredited time for good behavior. While the announcement at a civic club speech that we are going to eliminate all parole will surely bring prompt and sustained applause, it often has the opposite effect of its intention.

People are in prison largely because they failed to understand how life should work, with people being rewarded for hard work and responsible action, and suffering the consequences of irresponsible and reckless action. This is true whether we learn such a lesson on the playground or working for a company. It is fair to say that people in prison did not get there for singing too loud in church last Sunday but due to their unwillingness to abide by simple rules of common courtesy. The concept of parole is that an inmate can complete educational goals, be industrious, follow the rules, and get along with other inmates in order to earn his or her most precious commodity—time.

Imagine saying to an inmate, "If you act surly, do absolutely nothing to learn useful skills, talk back to the guards, and show no initiative, you will stay the entire ten years of your sentence. If, however, you learn a useful skill, exhibit normal social behavior, speak and act respectfully toward others, and show a spirit of cooperation, you will still serve exactly ten years." What kind of incentive is that? Yes, I believe in "commit the crime and do the time," but it is in society's best interest to have a system that keeps hope alive in the minds of violators.

Trying to implement a balanced and restorative criminal justice system is not without political risk. In my reelection bid for governor in

2002, my opponent stopped being just plain honest with the facts of some cases and tried desperately to distort my record. Her attempts to paint me as "soft" on crime were ultimately exposed as lacking credibility, given the fact that the crime rate per 100,000 population in the state had actually *fallen* nearly 14 percent during my term as governor, with 1,600 fewer violent crimes and 6,700 fewer property crimes, despite the fact that during the same period our population increased by 10 percent. It was also hard to make a case for my being too "lenient" when I had carried out the death penalty more than any governor in Arkansas's modern history.

Conflicts (Impediments to Restoration)

A little girl and her father were at the post office to purchase stamps. The little girl became absorbed in looking at the pictures of the FBI Most Wanted list displayed prominently on the walls. She asked her father, "Daddy, who are all these men whose pictures are on the wall?" The dad replied, "Oh, sweetheart, those are criminals, very bad ones that the FBI is looking for all over the country." "Daddy, if the FBI wanted them so badly, how come they didn't just keep them when they took their picture?"

There are many impediments to correcting our corrections system. Let me list four of them:

Community Attitudes

No issue seemed to stir more controversy during my tenure as governor than that of clemency. "Clemency" is a term that can refer to several actions a governor can take, including a full pardon or a reduction in sentence (or commutation). In our state, the parole process is entirely separate and a governor has no role whatsoever in a parole unless he reduces the time served by way of commutation so as to make an inmate parole-eligible. The parole itself is not in any way under the jurisdiction of the governor, but under what is commonly called a parole board, but in our state is known as the Post Prison Transfer Board.

Each state has different laws that apply to the process of applying for clemency. I was presented with an average of over 1,200 case files per year to review and consider for clemency. Prior to the file arriving to me, members of the Post Prison Transfer Board would review the applicant's record, conduct interviews with the inmate, victims, law enforcement, and prosecutors, and the members would then vote on a recommendation for or against an action of clemency.

The easy thing would be to simply deny such requests. It would, by far, be the politically prudent thing to do. No governor has ever gotten in trouble for denying 100 percent of the clemency requests that come his or her way. It gives one the ability to appear and even brag about being "tough on crime." While it would indeed be the politically expedient thing to do, I also felt it would be a complete dereliction of duty to routinely ignore the process of law I had sworn to carry out when I took the oath of office.

While I am not obligated to grant any clemencies, I genuinely believed that each one should be considered and decided on its own merit. I further realized that there was always the possibility of a mistake, and over the course of ten and a half years, I did, in fact, grant clemency to some who merited it. Fortunately, no one to whom I granted clemency got out to commit murder, but obviously anyone granted clemency who violates again can be a real embarrassment.

There is another side to clemency that gives a governor an opportunity to correct what may be an injustice, not only on the issue of guilt or innocence but in the case of an excessive sentence or in the case of a person who has overwhelmingly displayed signs of such extraordinary reformation that there seems to be no further purpose in continuing the punishment. As horrifying as it would be to let someone out prematurely who would go forth to hurt another person, it would be equally horrifying to think that we kept an innocent person in prison who had been falsely convicted or that we extended an unreasonable sentence simply because we feared the political consequences of doing the right thing.

Unfortunately, clemency cases are wonderful fodder for political campaigns. The complexity of a decision based on the review of hundreds of pages of a case file is easily overcome by a twelve-second sound bite or a thirty-second television commercial run by a political opponent.

The fact that so many people do not fully understand the difference between a pardon, a commutation, and a parole is something with which I became all too familiar during the course of perhaps one of the more troubling cases to ever come across my desk, that of convicted rapist Wayne Dumond.

Dumond had been accused of raping a Forrest City, Arkansas, high school student in the 1980s. The young lady, a cousin of then governor and future president Bill Clinton, identified Dumond in a police lineup. Prior to his trial, two men broke into his home, hog-tied him, and castrated him. They left him to bleed to death. Dumond was found by his young sons, who came home from school to find him lying in a pool of blood. The local sheriff, himself later to be convicted of felonies, proudly displayed the severed testicles in a jar on his office desk.

The rape victim was from a prominent family in the community. The case attracted widespread attention, as well as notoriety, because of the castration. Dumond's assailants were never identified or arrested. The trial ended with a guilty verdict, but was surrounded by controversy. The sentence given to Dumond was harsher than any sentence for a similar crime in at least a dozen years for that county. In 1992, while Governor Bill Clinton was out of state campaigning for president, Acting Governor Jim Guy Tucker, the lieutenant governor, commuted Dumond's sentence, making him eligible for parole. The governor did not have the authority to issue parole; for that, authority rested solely in the hands of the parole board, and required an approved parole plan with verification of employment and living arrangements outside prison. Despite being eligible, Dumond was denied parole each time he applied.

Dumond's file for additional commutation was sitting on Jim Guy Tucker's desk when I assumed the office of governor. Since Tucker had already commuted his sentence, making him parole-eligible, any further commutation would have reduced his sentence to time served, allowing him to leave prison immediately with or without a parole plan.

Prior to leaving office, Tucker had told me in a personal conversation that he had commuted Dumond's sentence because it seemed excessive in view of similar cases from that area and because of other concerns he had about the case. While there was speculation at the time that Governor Clinton was unaware that the commutation was going to take place, I know from my understanding of the inner workings of the process in the governor's office how impossible that would be. The commutation would have involved the participation of several staff members in Governor Clinton's office. It is unthinkable that an action of that magnitude could have happened without his knowledge, if not full approval.

By the time I first saw Dumond's file in September 1996, I had received information that gave me reason to consider commuting his sentence to time served. Per the Arkansas law, I announced my intention to do so. Subsequent to that announcement, additional information surfaced that caused me concern about his being free without any responsibility for supervision and regular reporting to a parole officer. Based on his exemplary prison record and the support that he had gained, and due to the commuted sentence from Lieutenant Governor Tucker, I supported his parole, but ultimately denied his request for a further commutation. It was my only official action in the Dumond case. A parole plan was eventually approved for Dumond, but two years later, he was arrested on a murder charge of a Missouri woman and suspected in yet another similar killing. He died in jail before going to trial and with his death, many unanswered questions remain.

Fueled by a tabloid story quoting very partisan political operatives—one of whom I had not reappointed to the Post Prison Transfer Board—allegations were made of a "secret deal" between the board and me. The so-called exposé in the tabloid did not question why the sources never made these allegations until weeks before a heated election, or why those comments were made while openly campaigning for my opponent. The fact that I had failed to keep the source in a lucrative job was also never mentioned. Nor was there any attempt to explain how a newly sworn-in Republican governor would have so much influence over board members appointed by two previous Democratic governors. That same tabloid would regularly speak of my "pardon" of Wayne Dumond, despite the fact that the only action I had taken in regards to his case was actually to deny his clemency. To this day, that tabloid has failed to even attempt to be honest with the facts.

Constraints of Resources
One of the serious challenges in seeking to reform the criminal justice system in Arkansas was that legislators, particularly my Republican col-

leagues, would often vote for extended sentencing, harsher penalties, and longer prison terms, but would not feel any obligation to provide the necessary funding to pay for the increased and longer incarcerations. Had it not been for the creation of the drug courts and a new focus on community corrections, it would have been difficult, if not impossible, to have ever met the budget given a growing inmate population and increased costs associated with it. To this day, I find it disingenuous of members of my party to vote for costly programs to keep people in prison longer but vote against the revenues to pay for them.

Constitutional Issues

In addition to the obvious concerns of making sure that the constitutional rights of the accused were protected, we also struggled with perhaps one of the most delicate issues of all—balancing a state-operated prison system with the incredible value of faith-based programs that help bring the inmates to a point in their lives where they are truly changed from the inside. Faith-based programs that focus on internal changes prior to external changes have been of extraordinary value. Those programs have been more responsible than any other factor for experiencing a true reformation, and not just "jail house religion." Government has the power to lock people up, but only a change from the inside sets people free.

Comprehensive Involvement

For there to be a criminal justice system that is ultimately based on restorative justice, it must involve making things right with the victim, as well as correcting the behavior of the perpetrator. There must be comprehensive involvement that includes the victims, the criminals, and the community, social services, law enforcement, the legal system, educators, employers, and faith-based organizations. Unfortunately, too many people prefer the out of sight, out of mind approach to those convicted of crimes.

Character

A congressional candidate was meeting with his political consultant and was asked, "Do you lie, steal, or cheat?" The aspiring congressman said,

"No, but I am willing to learn!" The ultimate reason people are in prison is their lack of personal character, as evidenced by their self-centered will to break the law and violate the moral code of society.

To those who would argue that addressing the issue of character is not a function of government, I would respond that the lack of character has become a very expensive part of government! That expense is evidenced by the budget of our court systems, the department of corrections, and the law enforcement agencies as well as the cost of stolen property and the increased insurance premiums to pay for replacing it.

The Arkansas prison system is run with amazing efficiency, especially compared to the systems of other states and the federal system. The average inmate costs $17,000 per year compared with the average cost of in-state prisons nationally at $22,000 per year. The inmates in our system all have assigned jobs, the system grows virtually all of its own food through its farming operation, and inmates make most of their clothing and perform countless hours of valuable community service.

While I am glad we have a prison system that can house those that we truly need to be afraid of, it grieves me when I think of how much I would rather have those folks in a university than a penitentiary. Maybe if we had been more diligent in their growing up with education programs that appeal to them, community mentoring programs to give them examples of proper adult behavior, and the simple encouragement to believe that their lives could be better at the finish line than they were at the start, things could be different. Most of all, if we'd focused on policies to help create stable families and strong fathers, we'd have much less of a problem.

While many of the efforts to reform the system have brought some measure of sanity to the process—drug treatment as opposed to merely warehousing drug users—additional efforts are necessary to prevent the kind of life that leads to a prison term.

Some people would not be willing to pay one dime out of each dollar to church and faith groups in the form of a tithe to reach kids before they turn bad. Those same people resent nearly fifty cents out of every dollar earned being paid in taxes in part for the incarceration of those we fail to touch in those formative stages of youth. Drug courts, day reporting centers, and day reporting programs are just a few examples of efforts that can be made to improve not only the safety and security of our streets and neighborhoods, but also to provide a greater sense of sanity to our criminal justice system.

In April 2006, Arkansas Department of Corrections Director Larry Norris and I flew to Guantánamo Bay, Cuba, to see firsthand the facilities and treatment of detainees kept as suspects for terrorist activities against the United States. Larry and I were amazed at the extraordinary efforts being made to accommodate these detainees in every possible way, from providing strict Halal meals conforming to their Islamic religion, accommodating their prayer times each day, and treating them with levels of comfort and true humaneness. These are not people who have any respect whatsoever for our laws, our culture, or our very lives. Most of them truly hate the United States of America and express their gladness when Americans are killed and their hope of more to follow. The remarkable men and women—our soldiers and sailors—who operate the facility that houses the detainees at Guantánamo are able to turn a deaf ear to the cruel comments said to them and about them, and the unspeakable degradations that are put upon them day in and day out.

Though I left with sympathy and respect for those who operate that center, I also was reminded that despite the fact that most of the world will not appreciate or even acknowledge it, the United States of America is still a place where we treat even the most vicious criminals with a sense of respect and decency.

12 Action Steps to STOP
the Revenge-Based Criminal Justice System

1. Sit through a morning of criminal court.

2. If possible, visit a prison or jail.

3. Attend a meeting of or visit with a member of Parents of Murdered Children.

4. Read *Justice That Restores* by Charles Colson.

5. Talk with a police officer about his job.

6. If you know someone whose child has a drug problem, ask them to share their story as parents.

7. Sponsor an inmate's child at Christmas through Angel Tree or similar program.

8. Make a contribution to a rape crisis center, domestic abuse relief center, or children's emergency safe house.

9. Check to see if sex offenders live in your neighborhood.

10. Be part of a neighborhood watch group or Crime Night Out.

11. Sign up for a Citizen's Police Academy.

12. Take steps to prevent being a victim of crime (alarm system, self-defense class, and so on).

Chapter 7

STOP ROBBING THE TAXPAYERS

Columnist Dave Barry has a wonderful solution to the complicated tax code based on the TV show *Survivor*. We put all of Congress on an island and lock their food in a box. The only person who can unlock the box is a regular taxpayer named Bob; every day that Congress rewrites a section of the tax code so that Bob can understand it they get to eat. If Bob cannot understand what they write, they don't eat. Whether they ever eat or not, Barry also recommends that we never let them off the island!

Mark Twain once said, "Everyone talks about the weather, but no one does anything about it." That is pretty much the way it is with tax reform; every person running for office or in office talks about it but rarely acts.

The real key to meaningful tax reform is not going to be found in the hands of the politicians, but rather in the hands of the people who at some point will be fed up enough to demand either a simpler and fairer tax system and more responsible spending on the part of Washington or a systematic change in those who serve in Congress. We need to give a new team some playing time on the field to see if we can score a few for the taxpayer instead of the tax taker.

It would not be so painful paying taxes if Congress didn't waste so much of what we give them. One of my favorite writers is P. J. O'Rourke, who over the years has said some provocative things. Being the libertarian that he is, P.J. has been an equal-opportunity offender. Some of the more potent O'Rourkeisms are:

- Politicians are interested in people; not that this is always a virtue, fleas are interested in dogs.
- Giving money and power to a government is like giving whiskey and car keys to teenage boys.
- The Democrats are the party that says government will make you smarter, taller, richer, and remove the crabgrass on your lawn. The Republicans are the party that says government does not work and then they get elected and prove it.

His comment about government waste is particularly relevant:

- It is a popular delusion that government wastes vast amounts of money through inefficiency and sloth. Enormous effort and elaborate planning are required to waste this much money.

Don't get me wrong. I know the Bible tells us to "render unto Caesar the things that are Caesar's," so I am not opposed to paying taxes, but I agree with what Arthur Godfrey once said, "I am proud to be paying taxes in the United States. The only thing is I could be just as proud for half the money."

According to the Tax Foundation, last year Americans worked 107 days, until April 17, to pay their share of federal, state, and local taxes. That is longer than we work to pay for housing, health care, food, clothing, transportation, recreation, and savings. We worked more days to pay our federal tax burden alone than we did to pay our food and clothing combined.

Another gem of wisdom from P. J. O'Rourke puts it in simple terms: "If government were a product, it would be illegal to sell it."

There are two distinct but connected issues relating to tax policy. One is how much we should collect and the second is how we should go about collecting that amount. As we wrestle with the questions of amounts and collection, the other side of the equation is to determine what we will do with the money once we collect it.

It has been my experience that the best way to solve highly complicated problems is to try to first determine how to express those problems in the simplest of terms. "How much money does the government really and truly need to do the things that it is required to do?" This is the concept of what is often called zero-based budgeting. When I first became governor in 1996, the biennial budget process was already under way for the 1997 legislative session that would set the budget for the next two years. My first budget instructions to state agencies brought no small sense of grief and alarm. Instead of simply asking, "What did you have last time and how much more do you need?" I asked them to define their essential functions and explain how they could deliver those with the least amount of resources possible.

This was somewhat of a shock to a system that for years had been based on the notion of taking a previous budget, adding amounts for inflation and proposed new programs, and calling that a budget. As Ronald Reagan once said, "The nearest thing to eternal life we will ever see on this earth is a government program." Giving birth to government programs requiring new expenditures is not that difficult. The true difficulty is turning off the life support when those programs are old, nonfunctioning, and kept alive artificially.

Taxes are a necessary part of funding a reasonable and responsible government. Taxing too little can result in financial imbalances and deficits as well as underfunding truly vital roles the government should fill, whether it is protecting our citizens with a strong national defense; ensuring that we have an adequate infrastructure to accommodate commerce, enterprise, and transportation; or having an education system that ensures that our people are well informed and prepared to take on the responsibilities of work. Families should be empowered to be self-sustaining, to prosper, and still have the capacity to contribute to those for whom disease or disability have made it impossible to perform at full capacity.

I vividly recall a meeting in my office with key members of my executive staff and our state's chief fiscal officer and his deputies who were responsible for helping prepare the state's budget. When I took office, the state was facing a moderate surplus. It seemed reasonable to me that if we had collected more money than was necessary to fund the budget agreed upon by the legislature, then it was a sign that we were simply collecting too much and the money should be returned to the taxpayers who had overpaid.

I asked, "When was the last time we had an across-the-board tax cut in Arkansas?" Our budget officer looked at his deputies and back at me and said, "Well, Governor, we have never had one!"

In 160 years as a state, we had never enacted a broad-based tax cut, but there had been numerous tax increases through the years. From the time I took office until the legislature convened six months later, I sought to frame the discussion in a different way than had been experienced in most legislative sessions where the discussion usually centered around "Which taxes are we going to raise and by how much?"

The new paradigm I wanted us to embrace was "Which taxes are we going to reduce and by how much?" In 1997, during the session of the Arkansas General Assembly, I had the pleasure of signing the first of several tax reforms in our state and the first true broad-based tax cut in our state's history.

Let me be both fair and clear. I did not, and could not, have done it all by myself. I entered that session as a Republican governor who had just taken over for a Democratic governor. I inherited a legislature in which eighty-nine of the one hundred members of the House and thirty-one of thirty-five members of the Senate were Democrats. I will always be grateful that when it came to reducing taxes and exercising fiscal responsibility, there were conservative Democrats in our legislature who were willing to work beyond their own party strictures to join with the governor of the other party to benefit the citizens for whom all of us worked.

During my tenure as governor, we were able to make the following reforms in our tax structure:

- Eliminated the income tax for families below the poverty line.
- Increased the standard deductions.
- Eliminated the marriage penalty, which had increased the tax liability of married couples who filed jointly.
- Eliminated bracket creep by indexing the income taxes to inflation, thereby preventing taxpayers from moving into a higher tax

bracket when their paychecks increase due to inflation or a cost-of-living increase that does not actually increase their disposable or discretionary income.

- Doubled the child care tax credit.
- Eliminated capital gains tax on the sale of a home.
- Passed the first broad-based tax cut in the state's history.
- Signed a property taxpayers' bill of rights establishing a uniform notice and due process procedure allowing taxpayers to appeal valuation and assessments.
- Provided an income tax credit for companies that provide or reimburse for training and education programs for employees.
- Cut the capital gains tax for individuals and businesses in order to encourage investment.

In my initial years as governor, I was fortunate that the economy was strong and growing. Over the course of my tenure we were able to enact some ninety different tax decreases.

Starting in 2000, accelerating in 2001, and then spiraling after the September 11 terrorist attacks in 2001 and on through much of 2002, state revenues—not just in Arkansas, but across the country—began to change dramatically.

Several factors affected our financial picture. The burst bubble of the dot-com craze had a dramatic national effect on economic activity and consumer confidence. The loss of manufacturing jobs to Mexico and China not only affected individual employees and United States–based companies but also forced states to launch efforts to retrain displaced workers and help educate and prepare them for jobs different from the ones they had lost. Medicaid expenses continued to soar out of control and were especially burdensome on states. Because Medicaid is an entitlement, states had little control, if any, on how much money they had to spend. Basic medical costs were rising at twice the rate of inflation on an annual basis. Additional problems with lost employment in the private sector forced record numbers of people onto the Medicaid rolls. Large increases in the number of long-term-care patients, due to an aging population living longer than actuarial tables anticipated, contributed to disproportionately large gains in the cost of state-funded long-term care. In addition, many states, including ours, were faced with significant court-ordered increases in education funding.

Meanwhile, policies enacted in the early 1990s to get tough on crime were beginning to take their toll on state prison populations and budgets. Record numbers of people were receiving and staying for longer sentences. If that were not enough, courts were often mandating expensive training or therapies to assist those in prison.

Most people in my own state never fully comprehended that almost all the state's general revenue budget was spent on three things: education, Medicaid, and prisons. Those three areas account for approximately 91 percent of our state's general revenue expenditures. That means that the rest of state government falls within the final margin of 9 percent, which includes the state police, regulatory agencies, and all administrative agencies.

Often sincere and well-meaning people would call talk shows and pontificate that if we would park a few state-owned cars, cut travel budgets, et cetera, we would be able to save vast amounts of money. While we made every attempt to force frugality in such areas, the truth was, and still is, that we could totally eliminate all the agencies in state government with all their expenses (with the exception of the monies we spend on education, Medicaid, and prisons), and we would save only 9 percent. Through 2000, 2001, and most of 2002, we kept the boat floating even though the water got quite low and we sometimes found ourselves dragging it over the shoals.

Over the course of two challenging years, we ended up cutting 11 percent of the state general revenue budget. Those were some of my most challenging days of governing. No elected official likes saying no, but we had to say no to many good and even desirable things in order to fund the absolute necessities.

Special interest groups and individuals affected by the deep cuts in our budget wrote letters, staged repeated protests on the Capitol steps and in the Capitol Rotunda, wrote letters to the editor, and told of gloom and doom during repeated phone calls to radio talk shows. Every town hall I conducted was full of parents who brought their disabled children in wheelchairs, even when we weren't cutting services for these children!

In December 2001, the call for a tax increase to restore all the cuts had grown to increased decibel levels. I was convinced however that those calling for the tax increase, while quite loud, still represented a minority of the citizens in our state.

While speaking to the Arkansas Farm Bureau at their December meeting, I responded to those who thought the time was right to raise taxes. I announced that I had established a special fund at the state level for those citizens who felt they simply were not paying enough in taxes and whose guilt was driving them to demand the opportunity to pay more. I had created the Tax Me More Fund.

The Tax Me More Fund was quite simple. Arkansas citizens who felt they were not contributing enough of their personal or business income to the state treasury could write checks and the state would be more than happy to receive their voluntary contributions. While somewhat tongue-in-cheek, I was serious in calling out some of the loud voices clamoring for more taxes with a clear challenge and the drawing of a line in the sand asking them to either put up or shut up. While many of them failed to shut up, most of them also failed to put up!

Everywhere I spoke I carried envelopes already addressed to the Tax Me More Fund. I would ask if anyone needed an envelope so they could write a check and make a personal contribution to the Tax Me More Fund should they somehow feel guilty for not paying enough in taxes and wish to voluntarily contribute more. I must have carried those envelopes to dozens of venues and speeches and yet not one time did anyone lift a hand and ask for an envelope. From 2001 to 2005, a total of fifty-six people made contributions to the Tax Me More Fund totaling $2,076.79. It was a very potent way of pointing out the total hypocrisy of the insincere vocal minority who proved by their failure to write a check that they wanted more taxes to be paid, but they wanted them to be paid by someone other than themselves. In 2001, the Americans for Tax Reform named me as Friend of the Taxpayer for December for exposing the phoniness of the more tax arguments.

By late 2002, when the recession was at its peak and revenues in most of the fifty states had plummeted, governors across America, both Democrats and Republicans, were faced with difficult choices. At the end of each day when a governor lays his head on a pillow, he has to know that the state did not spend more than it received. Our law requires a balanced budget and it's "balance the books or go to jail."

In Arkansas, cutting 11 percent from our state budget had taken us to the place where we were making life uncomfortable for some, but any more cuts and we would go beyond making people uncomfortable and would start actually hurting people and doing permanent damage. The only cuts left were to take drastic measures such as massive release of violent criminals, closing nursing homes and forcing elderly sick people to fend for themselves on the streets, or slashing education budgets, putting teachers even further behind in salaries and endangering the next generation of our citizens by providing them with an inadequate education. The ultimate body slam came in early December 2002, when the Arkansas State Supreme Court issued a final ruling on a school funding case that had originated in the tiny Lakeview School District in the Arkansas Delta over ten years and three governors ago. Their ruling declared that Arkansas schools were unconstitutional because they were not equitably or adequately funded. The court mandated that the state take immediate steps to provide equitable funding, which meant not just equal in amounts, but achieving equality in opportunity, regardless of cost. Further, we were to add funds for adequacy, meaning that not only were the pieces of the pie to be larger but the pie itself had to expand dramatically. Attempts to beat back tax increases were considered impossible and the choice facing our state was either to defy the courts (and in so doing deny students a level of education they deserved) or accept the responsibility for obtaining additional revenue in the most responsible way we could find. The situation was not unique to Arkansas, but ours was certainly made much worse by a court ruling that left us no option for further reductions in the areas that cost us most.

In addition to the court-ordered increases in spending for education, we had been on the losing side of federal court orders in Medicaid funding, which required us to spend more—not less—for the Medicaid program.

To help offset the impact of the state court ruling, I suggested bold changes in the structure of our education system that would have forced efficiencies that we had long ignored. It would have dramatically reduced the number of administrative units to force more money into the classroom and away from the boardroom. I was appalled at the amount of money being spent to administer extra small school districts, such as the one with 112 students in the entire K–12 district. Some superintendents were paid more to oversee a few hundred students than I was paid to serve as governor for the entire state! I further proposed that we would reorganize all of state government, reducing the more than fifty cabinet-level agencies to thirteen to eliminate duplication and waste in administration, which could now be combined into greater efficiencies through economies of scale.

It was my firm belief that prior to enacting tax increases, we needed to guarantee to our citizens that we were operating at the highest level of efficiency possible. I would consistently ask state agencies to find ways of reducing their administrative costs in order to spend their resources to service citizens and not the operation of the systems themselves.

Despite passing the government reorganization efforts in the Senate, we were unable to get the reorganization plan passed in the House. There was a total breakdown in leadership in the House of Representatives due to the brash arrogance of a handful of freshmen legislators who fought every attempt for efficiency and had the audacity to portray themselves as knowing more about state government than twenty-five- and thirty-year veterans. School superintendents lobbying daily in order to preserve their fiefdoms and jobs made the efforts toward reforming bloated administrative costs most challenging.

While I had gone on record and openly stated the need for additional revenues to meet the court-ordered challenge we faced, the ultimate solutions presented and passed by the legislature were less than acceptable. I was appalled that they were willing to spend too much money for too little reform.

In our state there are three options that a governor has when a bill comes to his desk. He can sign it, veto it, or not sign it and allow it to become law without a signature. A veto in our system is virtually meaningless, because a simple majority can override a gubernatorial veto. By this time there were still seventy Democrats and a few Republicans who went along with the Democrat leaders, so the simple math made a veto unsustainable. The tax measure was necessary to balance the budget, but it was still frustrating that the majority of legislators lacked the courage and will to take the more aggressive steps for reforming state govern-ments and education systems for efficiency.

I was not the only governor forced into a corner when it came to tax increases during this period. Several other Republican colleagues and Democratic governors as well were faced with similar challenges to bal-ance budgets that in most cases had already been cut to the bone and into the marrow. It was especially painful having some of the national anti-tax groups condemn us for doing what the law in our states required and what responsibility to our citizens demanded. I grew to lose a great deal of respect for some of these so-called think tanks who have the luxury of operating in their ivory towers in Washington. Issuing generalizations and characterizations that were inaccurate and misleading, it became appar-ent that while they could bask in what they perceived to be ideological purity, they did so as a means of garnering media attention to their cause and as a fund-raising tool to rally donors to their so-called advocacy.

Strong conservative governors across the nation were demonized for doing what they were elected to do: manage their states effectively and efficiently, but also to do it within the boundaries of the law. Despite the characterizations and accusations, the unvarnished facts are stronger than the simplistic sloganeering and bumper-sticker policy-making that formed much of the criticism.

As frustrating as taxation at the state and local level can be, the raised angst in the American population is clearly toward the out-of-control spending habits of Congress combined with an overly complicated and burdensome federal tax system.

The Tax Foundation's 2006 annual survey of U.S. attitudes on tax and wealth determined that support for federal tax reform has now risen to 80 percent of the adults in the United States. These adults believe that the federal tax system needs major changes or a complete overhaul. Addi-tionally, a majority of those surveyed say they are willing to give up some tax deductions in order to make the tax system simpler. Only 2 percent of adults surveyed thought the current tax system is fine the way it is!

With a growing federal budget deficit in the headlines, the 2006 survey included new questions about taxpayers being willing to cough up more to eliminate the deficit and balance the budget. At the time of the survey, the budget deficit was $340 billion, which would result in approximately $2,470 per individual tax return to balance the budget. When asked if they would be willing to pay such an amount to eliminate the deficit and balance the budget, only 9 percent were willing. The majority believed that paying the additional amount of money would not result in actually reducing the deficit but simply in increased congressional spending.

An average citizen's current tax burden is 33 percent of income. When adults were asked what should be the maximum percentage of a person's income going to taxes at all levels combined—federal, state, and local—the 2006 response was 15 percent, just under half the average tax burden. Clearly, what Americans think they should pay and what they are paying in taxes are worlds apart.

While changing the tax code would require an extraordinary political will and the expenditure of a great deal of political capital, not to mention a demonstration of raw political courage on the part of elected officials, the issue must be addressed not only for fiscal sanity but to help restore some confidence in the system from its primary customers, the taxpayers.

The four key criteria for a solid tax system would be for it to be *fair* (no winners or losers), *flat* (a rate that doesn't escalate penalties for productivity), *finite* (it's limited and has a ceiling), and *family friendly* (it undergirds instead of undermines the family).

Several years ago, a group of businessmen commissioned some of the nation's premiere economists to develop a model for the "ideal" tax structure. Economists and scholars from Boston University, Harvard, MIT, Stanford, and the private sector accepted the challenge to devise a system to bring sanity to the system of taxation in this nation. Over $20 million worth of research went into the project. The authors were not given instructions on what the final product was to be, but were told to start with a blank canvas and paint the masterpiece of tax plans. The result is what is known as the "Fair Tax."

I first became acquainted with the Fair Tax as I traveled on the campaign trail in Iowa, where I was often asked my views on taxation. When I responded that I supported moving to a flat tax that I thought would be fair, I would be told that the Fair Tax was more than that. Finally, I received a copy of *The Fair Tax Book*, by Neal Boortz and John Linder, and I read it once and then again. I've been a strong advocate since.

The Fair Tax would eliminate *all*—yes, *all*—taxes on productivity and income for both individuals and corporations. It would mean an end to income tax, tax on savings, payroll tax, dividends tax, capital gains tax, and death tax. A worker would receive his or her entire paycheck for the first time in their lives. Because we would eliminate the income tax, we would eliminate the IRS—actually close down that $10-billion-a-year empire and make April 15 just another beautiful spring day in America.

How can that work? By replacing a tax on what we *produce* with a tax on what we *buy*. What we would have would be a consumption tax paid at the retail point of sales.

Most people don't realize it, but when you purchase something made in the United States, you are not only buying the product, you are paying the taxes and operating costs of the company that made it. In this country, that amounts to an average 22 percent embedded tax on *everything* we buy! A tax that is hidden, unseen by the consumer. And when you seek to purchase something, you take to the market a paycheck that has been significantly reduced by the withholding taxes—that means the government takes your money before you even receive it!

If you are self-employed, you're in for a big shock when have to pay self-employment tax. In addition to the cost of your combined taxes on what you've produced (estimated to be at least 33 percent per person), Americans are deprived of over $250 million each year in lost productivity just complying with the tax code and dealing with the bureaucracy of the IRS. Pollster Frank Lunzt says that more Americans are afraid of an audit by the IRS than of being mugged! After all, the mugging lasts a few seconds and you are only robbed of the money in your pocket or purse. An IRS audit can last months or years and may cost you every dime you have!

With the Fair Tax, we end the underground economy. Illegal immigrants, drug dealers, prostitutes, pimps, and gamblers will pay tax just like you. The tax system will be transparent and assessed at the point of retail sale.

For the tax to be revenue neutral, the rate would be approximately 23 percent, which might seem excessive at first, but remember that the average American's current tax burden is over 33 percent of their income!

Because of the onerous tax structure we have now, over ten *trillion* U.S. dollars have been legally moved to offshore and foreign accounts. What would happen in our economy if we had $10 trillion unleashed in our market? Jobs would come back to the United States and we would become the tax haven of the world rather than the country from which companies and individuals flee. You would not be penalized for earning, saving, investing, buying and selling at a profit, or dying.

Washington lobbyists and many members of Congress don't immediately love the Fair Tax because it moves the power to *you* instead of them! There are over 35,000 lobbyists in D.C. every day—that is over seventy lobbyists for each member of Congress! They win; we lose.

But isn't a consumption tax regressive, exacting the most damage upon the poor or those on fixed incomes? It would be, if not for a provision of the Fair Tax. In order to prevent people being taxed for basic necessities, each American would receive an advance refund of the amount of the Fair Tax times the rate of poverty as defined by the Department of Health and Human Services, then divided by twelve. It essentially un-taxes the poor, the elderly, and, for that matter, everyone for their basic necessities.

In considering the power of capital to create jobs and economic growth, we cannot forget that the greatest capital is human capital. When people are chronically ill, undereducated, or consumed with worries about adequate housing or the safety of their neighborhood, the productivity level and potential of those individuals is greatly diminished.

As our nation continues to try to plug the holes in our economic ship, we must address the long-term concerns brought about by a Social Security system that is rapidly heading toward bankruptcy. A huge tide of baby boomers is starting the largest wave of retirement in our nation's history. As they retire, they will cease paying into the system and will begin drawing out in record numbers. It is not a pretty picture and certainly not made better when allowed to become a partisan ping-pong ball with neither side willing to acknowledge the urgent need to address it. Perhaps one of the lowest moments for the Democrats was during the 2006 State of the Union address by President Bush when the Democrats gave themselves a standing ovation for proudly doing nothing to help the insolvency to the Social Security system.

One solution is to encourage people to continue working into their late sixties or early seventies or even beyond. If we maintain the current tax system, we should increase their incentives to stay in the workforce rather than create incentives for them to get out. First of all, we need their capacities, abilities, and skills, and as long as they are working, even if they claim benefits, they will still be paying into the Social Security system and helping it stay solvent.

Perhaps it is time to increase benefits they will receive for delaying retirement. Currently the increase ends at age seventy. So let's give more to those willing to wait until they are seventy-two or even seventy-five. Giving baby boomers of retirement age an additional exemption such as a "working senior" deduction might also encourage these citizens to stay in the system for a longer period of time. Some boomers have done so well they don't even need the benefits to retire comfortably. One option is to offer them a tax-free lump sum to be given to their kids or grandkids when they die, which would at least delay some payments for decades.

Another option would be to give retirees an option for a one-time buyout of their Social Security benefits to be received in a tax-free lump sum so the beneficiary doesn't lose his or her benefits, but the government isn't obligated for the long-term monthly residual obligation. With baby boomers reaching Social Security retirement age at the rate of 10,000 per day, something must be done and should be done without the divisive politics of Washington making this about *them* and not about *us*.

Creating a sane and sound tax policy ought to be one of the highest priorities of Congress, and if the current Congress is unwilling to do it, then the American people should elect a Congress that will.

If there is a complete unwillingness on the part of elected officials to take the bold steps to propose ways to establish a simpler, stronger, and fairer system, then perhaps Congress could do with the tax system what they currently do with the restructuring of military bases. Instead of the BRAC (Base Realignment and Closure Commission), perhaps we should create a TRAC (Tax Reform for America Commission), a bipartisan group of economists and citizens, like those who created the Fair Tax, who would propose a reformed tax structure. This would give Congress, or even the American people, the direct opportunity to vote it up or down.

From my own experience of dealing with tax reform and the difficulty in balancing a budget during my ten and a half years as governor, I realize it is much easier to oppose than it is to propose or even dispose of ideas. We must elect people who are willing to show courage, expend political capital, and stabilize the finances of this country.

12 Action Steps to STOP Robbing the Taxpayers

1. Write your congressperson and senators and urge action on a simpler, fairer, flatter tax system.

2. Donate a tithe or more to your church.

3. Become familiar with the federal budget and how your money is spent.

4. Attend meetings of your city council or local county government.

5. Add up all the money you pay to government in various taxes—federal, state, local, sales, utility, property, Social Security, fees, and so on.

6. Run for office!

7. Volunteer in a campaign.

8. Take all deductions possible on tax returns.

9. Write a letter to the editor.

10. Read publications like the *Wall Street Journal*.

11. Keep receipts for tax-deductible items.

12. Avoid taxes you legally can, but NEVER *evade* taxes!

Chapter 8

STOP the Heat and Turn On the Light for Hot Issues

Early in my training for my first marathon, I began experiencing pain and soreness in my left ankle and foot. Stretched out on the examination table in the office of my orthopedic specialist, Dr. Richard Nix, I impatiently awaited the completion of his examination and review of the X-rays he had taken. I was deeply depressed, thinking (actually fearing) he would tell me that I was simply too old to start running, or that my pronounced flat feet would prohibit any thought of continuing the training.

Sensing my apprehension, he looked at me with a smile and said, "Mike, you are going to be fine. It is just some tendinitis and we can work on that. This is just part of being an athlete."

"What did you just call me?" I asked, unsure I actually heard what I thought he said.

"I said these are normal symptoms for an athlete, and that is what you are because only an athlete could train for and successfully run a marathon," he replied.

"That is the first time in my life I have ever been called an athlete!" I said, jumping up from the examination table and immediately feeling better than I had ever felt before. This was one of those rare times in my life when being called a name truly made my day. After being in politics as long as I have, I am accustomed to being called names, most of which are not printable in this book. Name-calling is often a substitute for meaningful and thoughtful adult-level conversation, especially when it comes to hot-button, controversial issues.

I learned long ago that I gain little when engaged in conversations with two different types of people. The first type is the person who agrees with me totally. That person adds nothing to the conversation except reinforcement of what I already say and believe. While I may enjoy fellowship with someone who says yes to every view that I hold, there is little to be gained from it. The second type of person I have little time for is the individual whose mind is so thoroughly made up they have absolutely no interest in hearing anything but their own opinion, typically contrary to mine.

Thoughtful discussion with sincere people, often holding a different point of view, frequently reinforces my conclusion that my own convictions are correct. That said, at other times I find myself realizing whether or not I agree, and I can readily understand that an issue may not be as cut-and-dried as I would like it to be.

Some topics tend to lead to a great deal of heat, but not always a great deal of light. Address a select crowd, toss in a few "red-meat" issues, and just about anyone can whip the crowd into a frenzy, bringing them to their feet during the speech. Highly controversial issues can inspire, even inflame, the audience. Of course careful selection of the topic and being on the right side of it is key to determining whether you will be carried out of the room after such a speech on the shoulders of the crowd or on a stretcher! I certainly would not advise making a speech to an NRA convention advocating confiscation of personal firearms. Nor would it be wise to address a Greenpeace convention and advocate drilling for oil on the Outer Continental Shelf.

Let's put on our flame-retardant suits and jump off into the inferno of some of the hottest issues of the day.

Immigration and Border Security

During the past ten years I have rarely seen an issue so completely divide people as does immigration. Interestingly, the divisions are not predictable along traditional lines of Democrat-Republican, liberal-conservative, urban-rural, or coast-heartland. The truth is it would probably be easier for all of us if the lines were drawn with some rational and clearly principled approach.

It is my view that before we can sort out what needs to be done regarding the immigration issue, we must first stop, take a deep breath, and be reminded why we are faced with this issue in the first place.

My personal approach to the issue of immigration begins from this single starting point: Every day I thank God that by His grace I was born in a country where people try to break in rather than break out! I start from the position of gratitude, knowing through no effort of my own I happened to be born an American citizen, automatically granted the incredible rights and privileges most people on the planet yearn for, yet for the most part never experience. In America, I have it all: the complete freedom of speech, the freedom to worship as I please, the freedom to travel within the boundaries of my country without asking the government's permission, the opportunity and full right to be critical of my government, and the ability to challenge it by running for the offices that govern it. I am especially overwhelmed that despite being born in the most humble of circumstances, it is still possible to go from the back streets to the main streets, from working in the stockroom to owning the store.

I have spoken to many different types of groups in states all across our nation and, invariably, I find when the topic of immigration is raised, so are the hackles of the audience. On one hand, though there are an estimated twelve million illegal immigrants in the United States, it hardly seems Americans should truly feel threatened by people who pluck chickens, pick tomatoes, make beds, wash dishes, or mow lawns. Others argue if that many people can get across our borders and remain in the United States, enjoying the benefits of our education and health care systems indefinitely, then we don't stand a fighting chance of keeping true terrorists from exploiting our borders, wreaking havoc, and committing acts of terrorism right here in America.

Even experts cannot seem to agree on the impact of having illegal immigrants in our midst. Economists at the RAND Corporation found the cost to taxpayers in providing government services to immigrants ranged from a deficit of $1,600 to a surplus of $1,400 per immigrant.

How can the numbers vary so much? They depend on which of the many elements are factored into the analysis. Even though illegal immigrants might end up having their children educated for free or be given medical assistance for which they never pay, there is also the side of illegal immigrants who do in fact pay taxes in the forms of sales tax, property tax for property they rent, fuel they purchase for their vehicles, even Social Security taxes though they may not hold a valid Social Security number. Since 1986, illegal immigrants paid an estimated $300 billion into the Social Security system, yet took nothing out of it. This fact caused some to suggest that illegal immigrants are subsidizing us more than we are subsidizing them.

Their contribution to the consumer market is also indisputable. Some 80 percent of what illegal immigrants earn in the United States actually stays in the country. The fact that they often take jobs at the low end of the wage scale helps stem inflation and keep prices for goods and services lower and more competitive than prices would be without them. John Kasarda, an economist at the University of North Carolina, surmised that illegal immigrants have "kept some industries competitive that would have gone to Mexico and China." While some Americans claim that they would prefer to pay higher prices for their apples, meals in restaurants, or hotel rooms, the reality is unskilled domestic labor gives higher-skilled workers more time to put into more productive, lucrative work, and therefore more leisure time.

Those perhaps most affected in terms of jobs would be male high school dropouts. However, even among this population demographic, the presence of illegal immigrants creates the very incentive for those dropouts to return to school, complete their education, and enter the workforce on a higher rung of the economic ladder.

What we can't do is simply turn our heads and allow our laws to be flagrantly broken, acting as if the economic benefits to consumers justify the utter disregard for not only our laws, but potentially our security. In the case of immigration, our laws are clearly out of sync with the economic realities of an indisputably global marketplace. It would be sheer folly to attempt to suddenly impose a strict enforcement of existing laws, round up twelve million people, march them across the border, and expect them to stay.

What does make sense is a revision of our laws, one giving those here illegally a process through which they pay a reasonable fine in admission of their guilt for the past infraction of violating our border laws and agree to strictly adhere to a pathway toward legal status and citizenship. In exchange, our government gains the capability to know who is here, why they are here, where they are, and whether they carry a communicable disease. But much of the national debate has become mired more in definitions than in a real solution.

The influx of immigration has exposed a serious gap in the American economy. The U.S. Department of Labor projects a need of close to eight million more low-skill workers in the next decade. This requirement cannot currently be met given that Americans are now graduating high school at a 90 percent rate, almost double that of a half century ago. As a result, our labor pool now consists of people too educated for the lowest-skill jobs and undereducated for the highest-skilled jobs in the professional realms of high-tech or medicine. As immigrant labor fills the lowest level jobs, it creates a natural economic pressure, pushing our population toward acquiring higher levels of education and marketable job skills.

I respect the fact that many people are sincerely concerned about the security of our borders and protecting our nation from terrorists slipping in. I respect, as well, those who hold an honest regard for the law and feel any violation is unacceptable. However, I would be remiss if I failed to point out that some of the passion I hear in the context of this debate is rather disturbing. I'm referring to passion that has nothing to do with regard for law or anxieties about security, but that drives some of the most inflamed emotions: the passion sparked by the unholy flames of racism. Not all people with strong convictions about this issue are racists. Not even most are. I don't see that as the issue in any way for the elected officials at the state or federal levels who have legitimate concerns for security as well as for fairness in laws and economic considerations for tax-funded benefits given to those who break the laws. But listening to the seething anger from some who call in to talk radio or from town hall meetings I have conducted leads me to the inescapable conclusion that some of the rage is fueled by prejudice.

The less self-confident people are, the more they feel threatened by

people who are different. When vast numbers of people begin to surround them, people whose color is darker, whose culture is different,
and whose language or accent is unfamiliar, there can develop a genuine
conflict.

I remember the firestorm I created when, in a speech to a convention
of Southern Baptists in Arkansas, I declared that in the South—unfortunately even in the churches of the South—major mistakes had been made
in the manner in which African-Americans were treated hundreds of years
ago. I pointed out we were still paying the price, reeling from the sins of
our ancestors. My hope was perhaps God would give us a second chance to
have a different spirit with the influx of immigrants, especially Hispanics.
Hopefully, we would be better capable of balancing a legitimate respect
for law and the truest and highest level of both American and Christian
citizenship by providing a welcome assimilation for those coming to our
country for the same reasons our own forefathers did. I must confess, had
the immigration quotas and restrictions existed at the time my own ancestors disembarked from boats arriving from Great Britain, they would not
have been allowed in. My blood is not blue, but my collar is.

While I accept the premise that people who break the law should
make amends, I also find it wrong to punish a child for the crimes of the
parent. Yet, in some application of our laws regarding immigration, we
do exactly this.

In 2005, I proposed a controversial bill to the Arkansas legislature that
would have allowed any high school graduate successfully meeting the
criteria for college scholarships to apply for those scholarships, regardless of the status of his or her parents. In the case of Arkansas students, it
would have required a child to have enrolled in our school system long
enough to complete the entire core curriculum of twenty-four credits,
including four units of English, four units of math, three of social studies, and so on. These students would have been required to have scored
the minimum standard on the ACT exam as well as meet other academic
and personal criteria. Even after meeting these requirements, the student would not be guaranteed a scholarship, but simply allowed to compete for those available. Tragically, some opponents of the bill claimed it
would *guarantee* free college for illegal immigrants and take scholarships
away from deserving Arkansas citizens. While this was clearly an absolute

lie, some opponents did not let the truth get in the way of the opportunity to stir the passions of those already seeking something to be angry about. Although the bill actually passed in the House of Representatives, it failed to get through the Senate, primarily because misinformation and fear ultimately won.

My disappointment was for the students who would have been eligible to compete for the scholarships, the very ones who had already been in our schools. Some had been there for their entire K–12 education. They had already proven their discipline and dedication by being in the top tier academically of their class. Because of their achievement and potential, they possessed the capability of attending college. Applying for citizenship would be a prerequisite upon receipt of the scholarship, once reaching their eighteenth birthday. These were children who could possibly have ended up being high wage earners, and therefore significant contributors to our tax base. The child's only crime was being born to parents who might not have followed our laws on immigration. Our state constitution already mandates that *all* children under age sixteen, regardless of their citizenship, attend our schools because as a people we recognize education for every child is in our best interest.

I must confess my own views on this issue are shaped by the highest laws of human behavior, laws beyond those of the current but ever-changing immigration code. Simply put: "Do unto others as you would have them do unto you."

Rational, reasonable, and responsible approaches to this issue must be employed. I realize on the finer points many good and decent Americans will disagree. I truly hope that we will ultimately govern not just on what the law is, but what it should be. We Americans have always been at our best when our laws reflect the best of who we are, and not the worst.

There once was a period in our nation's history when people of color were not considered people at all. One must only review the shameful and infamous *Dred Scott* decision of 1857. To this very day 150 years later we are still not completely over it. Our laws once forbade people who were black to vote or even eat in the same dining halls as whites. Passions similar to today filled the air as people clamored for our country to follow the law! In some cases when the law reflects not our best, but rather our worst, the true American spirit cries out "Change the law!"

Gambling

A television ad for a popular gambling venue screams, "Somebody is going to win!" What it does not say is, "A whole lot of people are going to lose!"

I realize people who enjoy an occasional trip to a casino, walking in with a specific amount of money and limiting themselves to gambling within that limit, are not much different from others taking a comparable amount of money and spending a day at Disney World. Personally, I have never put so much as a nickel in a slot machine, purchased a lottery ticket, or bet on a horse. Part of it is probably the influence of my church but most of it is that I am just not that interested.

What does interest me is government-operated games of chance that entice citizens to play while making ridiculously false promises about prosperity being just around the corner.

It is one thing to legalize and license certain games of chance and other venues such as racetracks. In these places, some skill is needed to successfully pick a winner. I have seen how popular lotteries are in many states. Some of those state's governors expended a great deal of political capital helping get them established. I spent a great deal of political capital fighting them. I still believe there is something fundamentally unseemly about the government owning and operating a gambling operation, all the while using some of the worst examples of false advertising to encourage their citizens to pay what amounts to a voluntary tax.

Even if I did not have qualms about gambling because of my own religious convictions, I would still come to the same conclusion based on economic grounds. In 1990, I served on the steering committee of a statewide group that fought the establishment of a lottery in Arkansas. Years later, during my tenure both as lieutenant governor and governor, I was frequently asked by reporters whether I favored a lottery or some other form of expanded gambling. For some reason, it seemed they believed if they continued to ask the question they would someday get a different answer. I can assure you they did not; it remains the same to this day.

Some of my views were also formed by the influence of a pair of Duke University sociologists, Charles Clotfelter and Philip Cook. Their book *Selling Hope*, published in the late 1980s, examined the impact of a lottery strictly from an economic and sociological perspective. Their study shattered the myth that lotteries are good for education by showing that, in the long run, lotteries only shift money and rarely create it.

State lotteries spend hundreds of millions of dollars on advertising. Amazingly, state governments are not subject to the federal truth in advertising standards. As a result, they often employ a level of deceptive marketing. In fact, if used by the private sector the ads might well be the basis for criminal charges.

In a New York campaign for their lottery, citizens are told all they need is "a dollar and a dream." Another state made the promise, "Chances are good you can be ten thousand dollars richer." What none of the ad campaigns revealed was that lotteries give the worst odds of winning in any common form of gambling. Rather than having a "good chance" of winning, lottery ticket purchasers faced an almost sure likelihood of losing. In fact, statistically there is a greater likelihood of being struck by lightning than winning the lottery.

Some of my heartburn over financing legitimate government programs such as education through a lottery is it helps breed the notion one can get something for nothing. This hardly encourages the kind of work ethic that makes America a strong and prosperous nation. A good day's work is still more reliable than a good chance wagering, and a paycheck is far more reliable than a lottery ticket.

Despite being prohibited by law, lottery tickets are frequently sold to minors. A survey by the Massachusetts attorney general found minors as young as nine able to purchase lottery tickets in 80 percent of their attempts. Seventy-five percent of high school seniors report having played the lottery, according to the National Gambling Impact Study Commission report. That same report also indicated adolescent gamblers are more likely to become problem or pathological gamblers.

Lotteries are the only state program actually setting aside funds to help treat the addictions of those who participate. In the state of Iowa, a percentage of gambling revenue is earmarked to fund gambling phone help lines. In 2005, that state spent almost $4.5 million to treat gambling addiction. While on one hand the state spends money to attract gamblers, it turns around and spends more money to treat the devastating ramifications of its own successful advertising.

Data suggests lottery play is heaviest among economically disadvantaged populations. When visiting states with lotteries, I have noticed that I rarely see a well-dressed executive type standing in line on a Friday afternoon to buy a lottery ticket. Usually the line for tickets is taken up with people who look as if they could certainly benefit from the win, but truly can't afford to lose. The tragedy is they will most likely lose. Hopefully they did not spend all their paycheck on lottery tickets and still had some money left over to buy food and clothes for their kids.

Sanctity of Life

Americans are overwhelmingly pro-life, even among those who claim they are pro-choice. This is clear because Americans inherently treat life as something to be protected and preserved at all costs. In the Sago mine disaster in West Virginia, thirteen miners were trapped after the collapse of a mine shaft. Randall McCloy, who turned out to be the only survivor, was rescued. At first the fate of the other twelve was not known. No expense was spared, and heaven and earth were moved struggling to open that mine shaft just because there was the glimmer of hope the other miners could be alive. Regardless of whether it is Russians stuck in a sunken submarine, mudslide victims in the Philippines, or hurricane victims stranded atop their roofs, we place a high premium on human life and go to extraordinary lengths to protect it. There does seem to be one glaring exception; if the life is still in its mother's womb there exists an argument over whether or not that life deserves our efforts!

I am not pro-life because I am in politics. It would be fair to say that I am in politics because I am pro-life. By no means am I a single-issue person, but on that single issue I am, and will remain, steadfastly consistent. This abortion issue goes to the very heart of what I believe as a human being and it is consistent with the American tradition of giving voice to the voiceless, empowering the disenfranchised.

One of my earliest forays into political campaigns was in 1984, when I worked on a citizens' initiative to help get on the ballot Arkansas's unborn child amendment. I served as chair of the effort in Jefferson County. The goal was to amend our state's constitution to declare that life began at conception and to require it to be the state's official policy to do all it was legally able to do to protect and preserve life. Prior to that time, each attempt to pass this amendment fell short due to electoral defeat or court pushbacks. Ultimately, we were successful when it was finally passed in 1988. During those efforts I became acquainted with a school-teacher named Jerry Cox, a fellow worker in the campaign, and Leon Holmes, an exceptionally bright "country lawyer." None of us had been politically active before, but this issue and the lessons we learned helped us to see the importance of staying in for the long haul. Today, Jerry Cox heads the most effective and solid pro-family lobbying entity in the state, the Arkansas Family Council. Leon Holmes was appointed in 2002 to serve as a United States district judge by President George W. Bush.

Even though Arkansas has been considered one of the most pro-life states in the country, successfully passing pro-life legislation through the Arkansas General Assembly had been virtually impossible prior to 1997. This was due in large part to a complete roadblock in the Senate Health Committee, a liberal bastion where senators saw to it that no matter how reasonable a bill might be, if it protected an unborn child, they would see the bill aborted before it would ever be allowed a fighting chance on the Senate floor.

The record I am proudest of in my tenure of over a decade in the governor's office is having signed numerous pieces of pro-life legislation, including a ban on partial birth abortion. Another bill established a wom-an's right to know, ensuring her consent to an abortion is an informed one, based on the same information she would be given if she were re-moving her tonsils instead of her baby. Equally important was legislation mandating parents be informed and provide consent before the serious surgical procedure of an abortion could be performed on a minor. (At the time, parental consent seemed appropriate enough to be required for a child given an aspirin at school, but not an abortion in a clinic!) We also successfully pushed through legislation requiring doctors to inform the mother that the unborn child will feel pain, and provide the option to anesthetize the baby prior to abortion. Further legislation provided immunity from criminal prosecution should a mother deliver the baby and wish to leave him or her at a hospital or other medical facility as an alternative to abortion or, as sadly sometimes happens, abandoning the infant in a trash can or somewhere else to die. We passed legislation creating the "Choose Life" license plate, allowing motorists an option to place on their vehicles a public indication of their preference for adopting children as opposed to aborting them. Finally, I was pleased to sign into law the Arkansas Fetal Protection Act. This law made it a crime to assault a pregnant woman and do damage to the unborn child. Prior to the passage of that law, an attack on a pregnant woman carried no consequences for the injury to or even death of the unborn child.

This bill had a personal side to it for me. In December 1999, I attended an event at the University Mall in Little Rock. While waiting for the evening's activities to start, I visited with a young lady working in the food court at the mall. The young girl was named Sarah, which happens to be my daughter's name. I invited her to come to the Capitol in February, and at the appointed time she came and had her picture made with me. Barely a month later, Sarah was murdered. She was also six weeks pregnant. The person who murdered Sarah was charged with her death, but unfortunately no penalty existed at the time for having taken the life of her unborn child.

A few weeks after the Fetal Protection Act was passed, a young lady in Little Rock was at home when three young thugs broke into her home. They brutally beat her, leaving her severely injured and tragically killing the unborn child within her. Because of the Fetal Protection Act, those young men were charged, not merely for an assault but also for the death of her child.

While I recognize that abortion is a very controversial and difficult subject for many and while I further respect those who differ with me on this issue, it remains one in which I cannot compromise my convictions. I must remain faithful to the idea that life is a gift from God and an innocent life should not be terminated by the decision of another person. While I have often heard the argument that such a decision is between a woman and her doctor, if that same logic were applied in other areas in society it could be argued that child abuse is an issue between a parent and the child.

Arguing the fetus is merely an extension of the mother is biologically incorrect. An unborn child is the product of twenty-three chromosomes from her biological father and twenty-three chromosomes from her biological mother, thus creating a unique and specific DNA code. A fetus is definitely not a mere extension of the mother, as if akin to an appendix or a kidney.

Ultimately this issue will not be resolved by the passing of laws, but rather through the changing of hearts as we culturally determine abortion is merely a form of birth control, inconsistent with our historic and traditional value placed on human life.

Ownership of Firearms

My position on the Second Amendment to the U.S. Constitution is as clear for me as the position held by most journalists toward the First Amendment. While I do not consider myself a "gun nut," I proudly own a variety of firearms and enjoy hunting as well as sports shooting with targets and clays. But even if I were not a hunter or did not enjoy shooting as a sport, I would still be a firm believer in the Second Amendment right of Americans to own firearms for self-protection and as a matter of principle.

In 1998, a few days after the tragic and senseless killing of a teacher and four students on the Westside Middle School campus near Jonesboro, Arkansas, I was being interviewed by Katie Couric on NBC's *Today* show. She intimated that mass murder on school campuses seemed to be confined to schools in the Deep South, where there existed a "culture of guns." (This interview took place before the Columbine, Colorado, shooting spree, which removed the notion that such crimes are limited to the South.) I assured her that yes indeed, hunting and the ownership of firearms were Southern cultural traditions. At the same time, murdering innocent schoolchildren was most certainly not a Southern tradition, and such violence was inexplicable and indefensible regardless of one's geography. When she continued to press, obviously hoping for some validation of her view that shootings on Southern school campuses were in some way connected to the fact that more people in the region owned firearms, I finally reminded her that a man by the name of Colin Ferguson boarded a train and coldly shot twenty-seven people before finally being subdued. That event occurred in Long Island, New York, where gun laws were among the strictest in the country, and gun ownership is significantly lower than in the South.

There are 700,000 physicians in the United States, and the number of accidental deaths caused by physicians per year is 120,000, making the accidental death rate per physician 0.171, according to the U.S. Department of Health and Human Services. Using that same logic, if there are approximately 80 million gun owners in the United States, and the number of accidental gun deaths per year among all age groups is 1,500, then the same calculation reveals the number of accidental deaths per gun owner to be 0.0000188. In other words, statistically, doctors are approximately 9,000 times more dangerous than gun owners. Not everyone has a gun, but almost everyone has at least one doctor. Yet, I hear no one suggesting we ban doctors because of how dangerous they can be!

We certainly should be harsh with those who abuse firearms by employing them in the commission of a crime. But abolishing firearms because there are reckless abusers makes as much sense as abolishing cars because some people drive while drunk. Most firearm owners are not only responsible but, because they know the true danger of a firearm, are exceptionally careful and safety-conscious. My own membership in the NRA is something that I cherish and value. This is not so much because I love guns but because I love freedom, and I believe to trample on one part of the Bill of Rights is to trample on all of it.

So-called hot-button issues occupy a lot of our attention and are genuinely important, but it's troubling that any one issue would be the one and only issue that matters to a person. I have regularly received mail from those who began their letters, "I have always been a supporter, but your position on (fill in the blank with a hot-button issue) makes me promise to never vote for you again." While I hate to ever lose a supporter, I've come to realize that one who would abandon me over a single statement or decision I made is a person who would abandon me sooner or later anyway. It's impossible to please everyone all the time.

12 Action Steps to STOP the Heat and Turn On the Light for Hot Issues

1. Attend a naturalization ceremony.

2. If possible, share a holiday or ethnic celebration with a family of a different culture.

3. Attend a firearms safety course taught by the NRA or your state's wildlife resource agency.

4. If your state has a lottery, ask for a breakdown of revenues, expenditures, and winnings, and compare inflation-adjusted dollars spent by the state before and after the lottery.

5. Take part in a March for Life.

6. Volunteer in or contribute to a home that helps unwed mothers.

7. Get information in your state about the estimated number of immigrants (legal and illegal) and try to read material reflecting various viewpoints on their economic impact.

8. Read C. Everett Koop and Francis Schaeffer's *Whatever Happened to the Human Race?*

9. Compare violent crime statistics among the states with strict gun laws and those that allow concealed handgun carry permits.

10. Ask your state wildlife agency for figures on how much hunters contribute to the economy and to the environment through their hunting licenses.

11. If you do own a firearm, take a hunter safety course or classes to know how to use and care for the firearm properly.

12. Contribute to your local right to life or family advocacy organization.

Chapter 9

STOP the Loss of America's Prestige at Home and Abroad

Is America an arrogant bully, despised by other kids on the block? Has our strength become our greatest weakness? Can we again become a respected big brother to other nations instead of being viewed as a bullheaded, brutish thug?

In the summer of 1973, I traveled to the Middle East on a life-changing and eye-opening journey with my soon-to-be college room-mate, Rick Caldwell. Rick and I had recently graduated from high schools one hundred miles from each other, and had become close friends a year earlier at Arkansas Boys State, a week-long camp environment where students operated mock government exercises. The annual event, spon-sored by the American Legion, was steeped in tradition, prestige, and a simple motto, "For God and Country."

During the course of our senior year in high school we visited each other regularly and talked often. We eventually cooked up a crazy scheme to tour several of the nations in the Middle East between high school graduation and entering college that fall. We visited Israel, Jordan, Syria, Lebanon, Turkey, Greece, Cyprus, and made a brief stop on the tiny Greek isle of Patmos.

Given the tension that existed in the world during the summer of 1973, just months before the Yom Kippur War and only a year after the

Olympic massacre in Munich, I have to wonder, "What were we think-ing?" More important, how on earth did we ever convince our parents to let us do such a thing?

For both of us it was our first international travel experience, and while we were part of a larger group of mostly adults, we were pretty much on our own once we got to each country. Having such an experi-ence at that time in my life proved to be more valuable than I could have imagined. I went without deeply formed opinions about the countries we were visiting and approached each experience with eyes and mind wide open.

One of my more vivid memories was exploring Beirut, Lebanon. We were fortunate to see this beautiful and majestic city before intense war and bombings robbed it of so much of its grandeur and glory. As we walked along the streets of a Beirut neighborhood, we stopped and watched a group of children playing. Some of the young boys, probably around twelve years of age, noticed us and came over. They didn't speak English and we didn't speak Arabic, but remembering that the second language of Lebanon was French, I thought it might be possible for me to recall a few phrases tucked away in my memory bank from the two years of French I had taken in high school. (Unfortunately my motives for taking French in high school had more to do with the girls who took the class than the language!)

I spoke a couple of sentences to one of the youngsters, who smiled and replied with much more confidence and fluency than I had. It was indeed a brief conversation and was communicated as much by facial expressions of smiling than complete comprehension of our common language. It was hardly a diplomatic summit, but it made me realize that beyond the barriers of geography, culture, language, and religion, there yearns in each of us a simple desire to be noticed and respected.

Years later while I watched television news film of the massive destruction of Beirut due to war, I couldn't help but think about that young man. Somewhere tucked away in some boxes of mine there was a photo of the two of us together and I have often wondered, "Did he survive the violence and killing?" If so, he would be in his forties by now. If he is still alive, I wondered what kind of life he's lived and what kind of attitude he has toward the United States and toward Americans.

The importance of that brief encounter at that particular point in my life was that it reminded me to think more about *people* than just *places* when I traveled.

Almost thirty-five years have passed since that experience and since then I have traveled to approximately forty countries and almost every continent of the world. I have viewed some of the most amazing scenes on earth, from the Egyptian pyramids to Mount Fuji, from the sophisticated streets of London to the saturated streets of India and Pakistan, and the bombed and battered streets of Afghanistan. In all of my journeys I have tried to spend more time looking at the faces of people and trying to understand their lives instead of simply looking at the landscape and soaking in the unique and often stunning view.

Because of Vietnam there was a great deal of resentment toward America and Americans in 1973. I remember angry looks and rocks thrown at our bus in Turkey and contemptuous stares and often curt responses from Greek shopkeepers. It was my first, but certainly not my last, experience that showed me not everyone loved America as much as I did or appreciated its strength or assistance to countries around the world. Even though it loaned billions of dollars in foreign aid, even when its military preserved the security and freedom of those recipient nations, it did not translate into respect or gratitude.

While I certainly prefer America to be safe and secure within its borders than loved and appreciated across the world, I would also like to think that we have more options. The preservation of our own way of life doesn't necessarily prevent us from having positive relations with others in the larger family of the world.

I am not so naive as to believe that all nations and all peoples will love, appreciate, or even tolerate the United States. We have to accept the fact that we are indeed anathema to many radical nations, particularly those led by religious fanatics. They would view peaceful coexistence with the same level of scorn as having a rattlesnake in the crib with a newborn. There is nothing we can do to appease nations who inherently hate us based on a blind and irrational worldview rooted in century after century of perverted principles of religion.

We should certainly endeavor to build positive and peaceful relationships with as many nations as are willing to befriend us, not only for the benefit of our economy but for the greater benefit of a stable and safe world.

I chafe when I hear the critics proclaim it is all our fault that America is resented across the world. That is nonsense. Nevertheless, we can't ignore our role and responsibility to work diligently toward an atmosphere in which the mention of the United States and its leaders brings smiles of approval instead of curses of contempt.

It is both fair and accurate to say that America is now the world's remaining true superpower in terms of its sheer military and economic capacity. The less vulnerable a nation is to military defeat however, the more vulnerable it is to the resentment and outright animosity of even those nations that could rightfully be described as allies. Steven Spielberg's film *Schindler's List* was a remarkable work of art, but also a powerful social commentary revealing the conflict between true evil and true good. One of the most memorable scenes from the movie occurs as Oskar Schindler visits the commandant of the concentration camp. The cold-blooded and conscience-seared commandant is revealed as one who actually takes pleasure in killing helpless Jewish detainees as a form of sport. As the Nazi leader contemplates killing a Jew carrying out the chores near a barn, he remarks to Schindler that he has the power to take that life. The clear implication is that he relishes the power not only to end another person's life but to do so without any accountability or consequence. Schindler shrewdly replies, "Power is when we have every justification to kill and we don't."

Oskar Schindler clearly understood a simple lesson of life, that the greater the power one possesses, the greater the responsibility one has. The more capable of exercising power, the more necessary it is to employ great restraint. Having the power to destroy and not using it reveals not only the strength of force but the greater strength of restraint based on the hope that force would be the last, not the very first, tool to be employed.

From the time we are small children and learn to play with the other kids in the neighborhood, we become aware that some kids are stronger than others and can run faster, jump higher, hit the ball better, and, if they should so desire, probably beat the daylights out of us! When the kid in the neighborhood with dominant power uses his superiority to demand his way, win at every contest, force others to run errands, and ridicule the weaker children, that individual may maintain his position of dominance, but he will be resented by the other kids in the neighborhood. They will never openly express it, but deep down they hope that one day he'll fail so he, too, can taste the turf of humility.

If a kid in the neighborhood with dominant strength and power doesn't lord it over the other kids, but instead is an encourager and positive enabler, he will be respected. If instead of seeking to show his dominance and superiority, he expresses leadership by going out of the way to serve the needs of others, he will not be viewed with resentment but with respect and appreciation.

A true leader shares his power rather than shows his power. True greatness is revealed by humility rather than hubris. A person actually in charge doesn't have to announce that he is in charge. Fear can be obtained by a gun, but true respect can only be earned by using one's strength for unselfish service. The most powerful demonstration of leadership is not a clenched fist of brute force but an open hand of humble assistance. This is the very model of leadership and strength expressed by Jesus, who reminded us that if we really wanted to be great, we must be willing to serve rather than to be served, and that the spirit of our actions is as important as the actions themselves.

I would never want to sacrifice one particle of America's power. Ronald Reagan was right when he led this country to unprecedented military strength. Our best defense is a military so well equipped and so well trained that no one wants to challenge it. Strength is a far more effective deterrent to war than is weakness, and the United States should never be timid nor apologetic for the development of the strongest military forces on the face of the earth. But with the development of strength and unprecedented power there must also be unprecedented restraint.

One of my hunting rifles is a powerful Weatherby .300 Magnum, capable of taking large game with a single shot. I have quite a few other firearms, even a simple Daisy BB gun powered by compressed air made most famous by the classic Christmas movie *A Christmas Story*. One can shoot hundreds of BBs at tin can targets and not be overly concerned an errant shot will do much damage. The consequences of misfiring a BB gun are relatively minor, but the consequences of misfiring a high-powered rifle could be catastrophic. When I load, aim, and pull the trigger on the Weatherby .300, I know I had better be certain about my target and absolutely certain as to what might be behind it.

A nation with America's strength and its military might must never point its strength in the direction of another country unless it fully intends to use it. More important, we should not only be aware of the immediate target but of all that is beyond that target which could be affected.

In military language, the term "collateral damage" is used to describe casualties that were unintended when a bomb or bullet went beyond its intended target and injured or killed innocent civilians. The death of noncombatants brings embarrassment or remorse to those responsible, but unbearable misery to those affected. Anger, resentment, and long-standing animosity and bitterness are deeply embedded, and no apology or amount of compensation can fully restore trust for many generations, if ever.

Sometimes war is necessary and military action is the only tool left to rescue a hostage, to restore order, to relieve mass suffering, to rebuff a despot, or to regain freedom. But as surely as a bell cannot be un-rung, a bullet, once fired, cannot be retrieved back into the barrel. The truest sign of real strength is sometimes waiting to pull the trigger until we know what the bullet will hit first, as well as what it will pass through before it finally comes to a stop.

There has been plenty of second-guessing as to whether the United States should have invaded Iraq. Historians will have plenty of opportunity to evaluate that decision. Regardless of where members of Congress now stand, in the days leading to our invasion of Iraq, there was a consensus from both Democrats and Republicans that Saddam Hussein did have weapons of mass destruction. There was a wholesale belief that he would unhesitatingly use them against the United States if he had the opportunity and would gladly assist and supply terrorists who sought to repeat the horrific attacks of September 11, 2001. He had already used the worst of war weapons against his own people! We shouldn't have been surprised that he would use those or worse against the United States.

It may well be that the intelligence on which the decision was made was incomplete or flawed, but had we failed to topple Saddam Hussein's empire and he had utilized weapons of mass destruction against us, or supplied terrorists with the tools to attack us, there would have been an even greater anger that we failed to act—not to mention the unbearable devastation of more innocent lives lost.

I have not been privy to the classified information made available to the president and members of Congress upon which our decisions were made. It is perfectly legitimate for there to be a debate as to our strategy in Iraq—our plans to turn it over to the Iraqi people and a clearly defined exit strategy. But it is ludicrous for people to suggest that President Bush acted with disregard of American lives, or that he casually or callously made the decision to send American soldiers into a war.

I visited our troops in Iraq, Afghanistan, and Kuwait in January 2006. What I saw with my own eyes was vastly different from what those eyes had read in U.S. newspapers and had seen on U.S. television. The commentary that I got from the soldiers who were actually sucking the sand of the desert in their lungs and putting their feet on the streets of Baghdad was decidedly different from the words that I would hear from commentators tucked safely away in well-lit studios on U.S. soil.

If our efforts in Iraq were futile and we were losing rather than gaining ground, it would have been "breaking news" to those who were actually carrying out the day-to-day duties of trying to bring peace and stability to that nation. From the American soldiers as well as from the Iraqis I heard the specific ways in which an increasing amount of responsibility was being transferred from our hands to theirs.

Almost four out of five troops from my own state's National Guard were or have been deployed during this war, most to Iraq or Afghanistan. One of my saddest duties as commander in chief of our National Guard is to make a phone call to grieving families to express our state's sympathy for the death of their loved one. Each time our adjutant general would call and inform me of a soldier's death, I would hope and verbally express my desire that it would be the last such call I would receive from him and the last call to a military family I would have to make.

Now that we have gone to Iraq, one thing is certain—we need to make sure that we finish the job and finish it right. If we were to pull out prematurely and allow tyranny to be restored to that nation, the ripple effect throughout the Middle East and the world would be profound. America would be exposed as a nation who had great power but lacked great resolve, making us more vulnerable than ever. Terrorists would view our lack of perseverance as our Achilles' heel to be exploited. We would be more vulnerable than ever to upstart and wannabe powers who would be willing to engage us in a battle they were convinced we would tire of, bringing greater division within our own country, and giving otherwise ally nations less of a reason to trust our commitments and believe in any of our promises.

By contrast, the successful integration of a self-determining democracy in Iraq is the establishment of a beachhead of democracy for the Middle East, and could be both a model and pattern of the value of people being free.

There are certainly those who complain that the establishment of a stable government and democracy is taking longer than expected. That is a fair criticism. Perhaps one error in U.S. policy was not being realistic enough or forthright enough with the American people about the length of time it would take for the people of Iraq to self-govern.

It seems to be lost on many Americans that establishing democracy in our own country has been at times an awkward and messy process, and after 240 years of practice we still have not completely perfected it! It should also be pointed out that even in our own "sophisticated approach" to freedom, it took 150 years for women to have the opportunity to vote and an additional fifty years for African-Americans to freely vote.

Yet from the very beginning of free elections in Iraq, women and men, in numbers that shame America in terms of voter turnout, proudly displayed their purple fingers marking them as voters, but also marking them as targets for insurgents who sought to thwart every attempt at a process of free elections.

The question for Iraq is no longer whether we should be there. We are there. Now is the time to clearly and firmly define our goals, and set a realistic timetable for accomplishing them. We must learn from our many experiences with the people of Iraq, Kuwait, Vietnam, Korea, Japan, and Europe in all our dealings in the global neighborhood. We must seek to use our place of prestige and power not to embarrass or intimidate our neighbors but to inspire and encourage. We have every right to be proud of our nation, our heritage, and the prosperity we have achieved. However, we must also understand that while an appropriate level of pride is a noble thing, we must never erase the thin line between that appropriate pride and the raw arrogance that comes from failing to see life through any eyes but our own.

I have visited Israel nine times, and strongly believe in its right to exist and the important example it has set forth in its seriousness toward its own security as well as the admirable expectation it has of its people to be stakeholders in its preservation. Even though I support Israel, its boundaries, and its future, and believe its alliance with the United States is one of great strategic value, a conversation with a Palestinian reminded me that we must always realize most of life's important issues are not as simple as we would have them be.

The Palestinian, with whom I visited in Israel in 1984, was but a few years older than me. He told me about the day he came home from school and was met at the corner a block from the home he had known since birth. He was told that he didn't live there anymore. He was told that he would be relocated to a Palestinian camp and that his neighborhood, street, and home would be occupied by the Israelis.

It was always easy for me to understand why the Jews, having been displaced for thousands of years, would feel a divine right to return to the land promised to their forefathers and previously taken from them, but that encounter with the Palestinian also taught me an important lesson. He reminded me that even when we believe that the Jews have a God-given right to reclaim land given to their ancestors and taken away from them, there are still human beings who deserve to be treated respectfully and thoughtfully since they personally have not done wrong and now are being forced from what has been their home.

In many disputes the lines aren't pure and pristine and none of the solutions are perfect. We will take our sides, we will make the best judgments we can, we will seek to bring justice, equity, and fairness to all, but will painfully and humbly realize that we are unable to right all the wrongs or fully satisfy all the parties.

It would be wrong for Americans to pompously proclaim that all we have ever done and will ever do is right. That kind of arrogance will breed enmity and even alienate our friends. Neither should we hang our heads and apologize for our strength, nor retreat from our role as a beacon of light and freedom.

In some ways the level of resentment aimed at the United States is our badge of honor, especially when it comes from those who hate us more because of what *they don't have* rather than what *we do*. It's important that as a nation we seek to be an example, not just of strength, but of servanthood and that we demonstrate what it means to be a benevolent big brother more than a brutish big bully.

In the summer of 2006 as part of a trade mission to Asia, I had the opportunity to visit the DMZ along the 38th parallel separating South and North Korea and to stand on the side of freedom with my foot on the border of tyranny. North Korean soldiers stared from their guard positions with contempt. North Korea is a modern-day tragedy. It's a nation led by a lunatic despot who has starved, abused, and intimidated the people of his nation with propaganda and oppression. Their economy is virtually nonexistent, and their future is bleak. Behind me was South Korea, which is nothing short of a modern-day miracle. South Korea was a nation not unlike North Korea fifty years ago, but a growing democracy, personal freedoms, and a focus on education have helped it to grow into the tenth largest economy in the world. Never have I been so moved to see the stark difference between freedom and totalitarianism as I was at Panmunjom.

Every day I live, I give thanks that through no effort of my own, but surely by the grace of God, I was born in the United States of America. The blessings I have and often take for granted should never be something that I feel guilty about, but rather feel grateful for. We cannot force other nations to accept, appreciate, or even respect our way of life and our pride in it, but we can do everything possible to be as President Ronald Reagan once said, "a shining city on a hill," a symbol to other nations of strength and freedom.

12 Action Steps to STOP
the Loss of America's Prestige
at Home and Abroad

1. Monitor news and events around the world.

2. Travel abroad.

3. Attend ethnic cultural festivals.

4. Take a foreign language class at your local college.

5. Read extensively about other nations, governments, and cultures.

6. Become acquainted with families from other nations at your workplace, church, or neighborhood.

7. Host an exchange student.

8. Host an international family through a sister cities program or similar international exchange group.

9. Eat at International House of Pancakes (just kidding—wanted to make sure you were really reading the list!).

10. Attend lecture series or speeches by international guests in your area.

11. Have a current map or globe and become familiar with the countries mentioned in news reports.

12. Talk to an American military veteran who has served in Iraq or Afghanistan.

Chapter 10

STOP MOVING THE LANDMARKS
OF LIBERTY

Saturday, March 1, 1997, is a day I will never forget. That morning I had accompanied officers from the Arkansas Game and Fish Commission into the woods of Perry County to locate hibernating bears previously equipped with special radio-transmitting devices. Almost immediately, we tracked a hibernating bear to her den, made sure that she was thoroughly tranquilized, and then watched as a wildlife specialist examined the 350-pound sow as a part of a program to better understand the growing bear population in Arkansas. Fortunately for us all, the bear stayed asleep!

It would have been a memorable day on its own had the bear been the only ferocious thing I encountered. But it wasn't to be. During the drive back to Little Rock I mentioned to the state trooper who was driving, "This sure feels like tornado weather."

The sky grew darker, and the air got thicker. It was the kind of atmosphere I had experienced once before in my life. When I was eleven years old, a tornado came through my neighborhood in Hope, whipping shingles from our little rented home, whirling debris throughout the neighborhood, and scaring the daylights out of my sister and me as we frantically raced through the house trying to remember whether to open windows and doors or close them.

By the time I arrived in Little Rock, weather bulletins were already announcing warnings of possible storms, including tornadoes, moving in the traditional pattern from the southwest to the northeast. Two hours later the first of a series of phone calls came, advising me that a massive tornado was on the ground in Arkadelphia. During the next few hours reports poured in from all over the state. The calls revealed that a series of tornadoes, some reaching the maximum F5 level, had torn their way from the extreme southwest corner of the state along a path of almost 250 miles to the far northeast corner, before finally heading into Missouri. By day's end, a number of people were dead, scores were injured, and our state had experienced its worst single day of tornadoes in history as judged in terms of overall scope of property damage and physical impact to the state.

That the hardest-hit community was Arkadelphia was of personal concern to me. Not only was Arkadelphia the first town my wife and I called home in the 1970s during our student days at Ouachita Baptist University, but our older son, John Mark, was currently a student there and we were desperately seeking to make sure he was okay.

Two days later I accompanied President Bill Clinton on Marine One as we flew over the affected area. We landed and walked through what little was left of the once peaceful downtown district of the community of Arkadelphia. The destruction was beyond description. Virtually the entire downtown area was leveled, leaving behind a rubble of brick, insulation, and splintered wood. I have never witnessed anything like it before nor since in terms of total and complete destruction. It looked to me as if a fleet of B-52 bombers had carpet-bombed it completely. Standing at a familiar intersection in the downtown area and looking in all directions—north, south, east, and west—I was chilled at being unable to recognize a single visible landmark. For a few moments, I found myself disoriented by the lack of familiar reference points. It reminded me how familiar landmarks are indispensable in maintaining one's orientation and sense of balance. The lack of anything familiar in any direction is the ultimate experience of what it means to be lost. This is true not just of physical landmarks but of those key intangible common beliefs that define us as a nation, such as life, liberty, and the pursuit of happiness.

America's sense of well-being and her capacity to steady herself through the storms is directly tied to being able to reference her landmarks of liberty. No matter what has occurred, these have always made it possible for her to get back on her feet and regain her balance. If those landmarks are obliterated, as a nation we will lose our equilibrium and become hopelessly and helplessly lost.

Over the course of a generation we have seen a dramatic shift in attitudes and reflections within our culture. We have witnessed a transition . . .

- From *Leave It to Beaver* to *Beavis and Butt-Head*.
- From Norman Rockwell to Robert Mapplethorpe.
- From the Gideons giving Bibles to fifth graders to school nurses giving condoms to eighth graders.
- From fathers taking their sons hunting to sons hunting urban streets for their fathers.
- From drive-in movies to drive-by shootings.
- From Cracker Jacks to crack cocaine.
- From teens holding hands to teen mothers holding babies born out of wedlock and into poverty.
- From parents who believed their greatest responsibility was to lay down their lives for their child to the culture of abortion, where women march for the right to lay down the life of their child for college, career, or convenience.
- From children worried about getting As in school to teenagers worried about getting AIDS from sexual partners.
- From parents fearing their child might be the victim of a thrown rock at school to parents fearful that their children might be the victim of a mass shooting at school.
- From letting the air out of a teacher's tires to a teacher being knifed in the hallway.
- From a time in which teachers carried paddles and kids carried books to teachers carrying Mace and kids carrying guns.

Carle Zimmerman outlines eight patterns of behavior pointing to the fall of a culture in his book *Family and Civilization*. The patterns are:

1. Marriage loses its sacredness and divorce becomes prevalent.
2. The traditional meaning of the marriage ceremony is lost.
3. The feminist movement is strong.
4. Increased public disrespect for parents and authority.
5. Increased juvenile delinquency, promiscuity, and rebellion.
6. Refusal of people with traditional marriages to accept family responsibilities.
7. A growing desire for and acceptance of adultery.
8. Increased interest in perversions and sex-related crimes.

While the words of Zimmerman certainly sound as if they could be describing events from the front page of today's paper, he actually wrote his book in 1947!

Going even further back in time, we can learn a few lessons from ancient Rome. In the classic work *The Decline and Fall of the Roman Empire*, Edward Gibbon noted five reasons for the fall of Rome:

1. The undermining of the dignity and sanctity of the home.
2. Increasing taxes and spending public money on bread and circuses.
3. A mad craze for pleasure with sports becoming more exciting and more brutal.
4. The building of gigantic armaments when the real decadence is within.
5. The decay of religion, with faith becoming mere form.

The parallels between what Gibbon described as Rome unraveling have a chilling similarity to what appears to be the loss of landmarks in our own nation. To categorize Gibbon's observations, we could call them major shifts in the landmarks of *family, finance, folly, force,* and *faith*.

Family

Some of the most heated debates in our nation occur over the attempt to redefine the word family. While "family" has traditionally and historically meant persons related by blood, marriage, or adoption, there exists a relentless effort to redefine family to include any two or more people who choose to designate themselves as "family." Volumes have been written on "the changing family." Such a topic begs asking, "What are those changes, who made them, and what are the results of them having been made?"

A few days before Christmas 1988, when our now thirty-year-old son was twelve, we needed to make a family shopping trip. John Mark, the eldest, begged to stay home, insisting he would be fine if we went shopping without him, taking only David and Sarah. Given that he was prone to provoking his brother and sister on such outings, the family decision was unanimous! John Mark would stay home and the rest of us would make the outing.

Upon our return a couple of hours later, an excited John Mark met us at the door and announced that while we were shopping he had made a cake for the family. His expectation was for me to be the first to have a piece of the cake he so proudly made. My first reaction was one of genuine joy as I thought about his having spent time alone thinking of doing something nice for the rest of us. I told him I would be delighted to have a piece of the cake he had made. As he went about putting that first piece on a small plate for me to enjoy, I thought how this would be a great opportunity for me to engage in some very positive "dad talk." No matter how the cake tasted, I should be quick with praise and affirmation.

He brought over to me what looked like a normal piece of chocolate cake. I commented on how good it looked, put my fork into the cake and took that first big bite. I was already envisioning that the first thing out of my mouth after the taste of cake would be words of praise and gratitude for his efforts and thoughtfulness.

Unfortunately for John Mark, and me, the first thing out of my mouth was the cake! It was truly the worst-tasting cake I had ever had or hope to ever have again.

My first thought was perhaps he was trying to kill me; maybe he heard his mother say how much life insurance was on my head and how well off the family could be if they got rid of me. It was at that precise moment I started thinking about the man who, when asked how much life insurance he had, remarked, "I don't have any and I am not going to get any!" When asked why, he replied, "Because when I die, I want it to be a sad day for everybody!"

I was thinking maybe that gentleman had the right idea.

The expression on John Mark's face, however, let me know the cake's utterly reprehensible taste was not intentional. Quickly trying to recover from my unexpected reaction I said, "Well it sure looked good. John Mark. Did you use a recipe?" With a hurt look still on his face he replied, "Yes, Dad, I did." When asked if I could see the recipe in question, he quickly delivered it. The recipe appeared to be a typical and ordinary recipe for chocolate cake. I asked if he had followed the recipe exactly as it had been printed. "Yes, sir," he replied. "I did just what it said. But there was one thing that I did not understand. The recipe called for a dash of salt. I wasn't sure what a dash meant, so I put a *cup* of salt in."

In case you are wondering, you do not want to eat a cake made with a full cup of salt. It might be fine if you have cows that could lick it, but if you are used to enjoying cake, one prepared with a cup of salt will not be like anything you ever tried before.

My son had not set forth with a goal of creating a disaster; in fact he was sincere, truly motivated, industrious, and holding the best of intentions. Yet, despite all those virtuous motives and actions, the end result was utter failure. The reason the cake project failed was that when he did not understand the definition of a "dash," he made up his own definition and created his own standard of measurement.

Sincerity, hard work, and pure motivations are all admirable. But when we seek to make up our own definitions about life, family, marriage, or children, the results can be as disastrous as chocolate cake made with a cup of salt.

My boyhood pastor often said, "If you don't stand for something, you will fall for anything." Defining the family to mean anything ultimately means it represents nothing. The absence of moral absolutes certainly sounds like an admirable way to practice tolerance through consideration of others and open-mindedness, but attempts to redefine the family bring about confusion and chaos. If the term "family" cannot mean something, it will ultimately mean nothing. Those who wish to redefine the term "marriage" to include any two or more adults entering into some type of contract are not merely stretching an old definition for a new culture but are wreaking havoc on the institution of marriage itself.

Whether or not our culture should accommodate persons of the same gender who wish to share hospital visitation rights, insurance benefits, and so forth is an entirely different discussion, but to call anything and everything a "marriage" is unacceptable because marriage means something specific—a permanent relationship between a man and woman for life.

In America, people have the right to live as they please so long as they do not infringe upon the rights of others. But they do not have the right to redefine the basic terms of society without the entire society discussing and ultimately deciding. Should society determine they shall keep the historic and traditional definitions intact, then it must not be viewed as a sign of intolerance or hatred, but rather a simple recognition of preserving established standards.

Arkansas, like many other states, found it necessary to amend its Constitution to affirm marriage as a willful decision between one man and one woman to mate for life. The amendment was not passed to be "anti" anything, as opponents suggested. Contrary to that notion, the "anti" movement is actually one that attempts to overturn a well-grounded norm and established institution. By wanting to change marriage to meet their personal behavior, such persons are actually anti-marriage. I respect the rights of those who would attempt to make the change, but only if they are willing to respect the will of the overwhelming majority when the proposed change is rejected.

In state after state, Americans have clearly and consistently affirmed they want the traditional definition of marriage to stand. I only wish that Americans seek to define marriage not only in a traditional sense but also seek to express marriage in a more conventional manner through truly recognizing it as a sacred relationship, seeking to do everything possible to maintain that marriage for a lifetime. The only thing as troubling as redefining marriage is defiling it with halfhearted commitments, infidelity, and divorce.

The idea of no-fault divorce became prevalent and increasingly popular in the early 1960s. Laws in most states were changed, making it much easier to get out of a marriage, no longer requiring specific grounds or reasons to terminate what had once been a lifelong commitment on the part of two people. In most states, it actually became easier to get out of a marriage than to get out of a contract for the purchase of a used car! The results have been disastrous, with ever increasing divorce rates now hovering near the 50 percent mark.

Another affront to the sanctity of marriage is the growing use of the prenuptial contract, particularly among the wealthy or celebrities, which in essence is building into the marriage relationship a clause acknowledging the inevitable, unnatural end of, or the lack of permanence in, the marriage.

Divorce sometimes is indeed inevitable, especially when one party in the relationship refuses to honor his or her vows, is abusive, or abandons the spouse. More often than not, however, marriages fail because of impatience or mounting pressures related to finance, stress, or other external influences. When divorce is easy, marriage doesn't have to be taken as seriously, since the couple may not really see marriage as a true "until death" commitment.

I proudly signed a piece of legislation to help stem the tide of divorce, especially when children are involved, by giving divorce court judges the option of mandating mediation when the dissolution of the marriage involves children. While the law does not prohibit the divorce, it would at least force the parties to heed a judge's order to try and work out details related to children. Hopefully, this will help prevent children from becoming the weapons of choice in the ongoing battle between two people who once loved each other.

Another bill I signed was legislation making Arkansas the third state in the nation to give couples the option of entering into what is commonly known as a "covenant marriage." As a result of the provisions, on Valentine's Day 2005, my wife and I were able to renew our own marriage vows and convert our marriage license to a covenant marriage license. We did this in front of nearly nine thousand people in the ALLTEL Arena in North Little Rock, using this "covenant marriage event" in Arkansas as a way of encouraging others to consider exercising this option either as a conversion of their existing marriage or when entering into marriage.

As one can imagine, some cynics sought to entertain themselves by belittling the concept of covenant marriage. By ignorance or intent, they totally mischaracterized what it really meant.

A covenant marriage is not, as critics suggested, a "super-sized" marriage. It is not intended to make marriage better, bigger, or more biblical. In fact, covenant marriage is the polar opposite of professing one's marriage to be "better." It is the honest acknowledgment of the fact that marriage is hard work and, under even the best of circumstances, difficult to maintain. It is the acknowledgment of the frailty of our human existence and the selfishness with which we approach everything. Covenant marriage simply means the two parties agree that before they get a lawyer and seek to get *out* of their marriage, they legally promise they will first see a counselor and try to stay *in* their marriage.

The covenant marriage can still be dissolved, but there are speed bumps to slow down the process so a couple can contemplate whether the dissolution of the marriage is really the best course. Obviously, couples may still divorce when there is abuse, abandonment, addiction to drugs or alcohol on the part of a spouse, or adultery in which the honor of one spouse is violated by the selfishness of the other. Those conditions do not force the divorce, but comprise the conditions under which it could take place without there being an extended waiting period. It expressly does not, as was falsely asserted by some, force people to remain in dangerous and abusive relationships.

As a result of the passage of this bill, many clergy in our state declared their intention to perform only covenant marriages in their churches, synagogues, or places of worship in the hopes it could help stem the tide of unnecessary divorce. Prior to my service as an elected official, the several years I spent in church-related service necessitated I spend a great deal of time counseling literally hundreds of couples going through marital crisis. My conclusion was that the only real winner in the divorce was the attorney, who was paid a handsome fee for bringing an unnatural end to what was intended to be a relationship lasting until "death do us part."

Finance

Having already addressed the issue of excessive taxation and foolish, unjustified government spending in an earlier chapter, I won't repeat all the points again. But I would like to reiterate one of the most important principles a public official should adhere to is remembering every dime spent from the public treasury is money that belongs to the people, not to the public officials who do the spending. Jean-François Revel, a French philosopher (and, as a communist, hardly a conservative, evangelical Republican), had it right when he wrote of this in his revealing book *How Democracies Perish*. According to Revel, the ultimate reason a democracy collapses is because its leaders discover that they can vote themselves benefits from the public treasury. Once their appetite for those benefits exceeds the ability of the people to pay, the system collapses from within.

The biggest fights I have witnessed in the legislature happen over the allocations of money, stemming from the politicians' scramble to show themselves most generous with money from the public treasury. Abraham Lincoln reminded us, "A government which can give everything can also take everything."

The true purpose of government is protecting its people, not providing for all of their wants. Many government safety nets have been created and now are largely necessary because of the failure of families to take care of family members, and the failure of the faith community to do its job in providing charitable assistance. Many Americans resent paying nearly fifty cents out of a dollar in various forms of taxation, feeling many government programs are wasteful and inefficient. At the same time, those same individuals refuse to give their God one dime out of each dollar in a traditional tithe, money that would most likely provide benevolence to America's needy. If such generosity were practiced by all, the government would not need to provide these benefits with tax dollars.

Our economic structure was based on the idea that our rewards should be directly proportionate to the risk we are willing to take. Those putting forth their own, or borrowed, capital and endeavoring with great diligence to put in the hard work behind their dreams should be able to enjoy the fruit of their labor, the prosperity of their perseverance. America's economy has been made strong by visionary entrepreneurs, individuals who took extraordinary risk, often investing everything they had and all they could borrow to bring an idea or product to the marketplace. Their success should garner our congratulations and thanks, not our scorn. Punitive tax policies that exact increasing proportions of income based on the level of success are a way of penalizing those whose ideas, innovation, or hard work has caused them to prosper.

I once heard the various forms of government described this way:

Communism—you have two cows and the government takes both cows and gives you part of the milk.
Socialism—you have two cows and the government takes one of the cows and gives it to your neighbor.
Fascism—you have two cows and the government takes both cows and sells you the milk.
Nazism—you have two cows and the government takes both cows and shoots you.
Bureaucracy—you have two cows, the government takes both cows, shoots one, milks the other, and pours the milk down the drain.
Capitalism—you have two cows, you sell one and you buy a bull!

Our system, based on the capitalist idea, is intended to create incentives so there is a return on one's endeavors. It has its flaws, but ours is still better than any other system on earth.

Folly

Edward Gibbon's depiction of the mad craze for pleasure, with sports becoming more exciting and brutal, could easily be a description of today's pleasure-crazed society. We are long past the simple, vicarious thrills we gained by indulging ourselves in observing others play contact sports such as football. When I was a child, Major League Baseball would telecast the "Game of the Week" each Saturday. Today, we have a proliferation of reality television. We are treated to productions showing the most bizarre forms of adventure involving supposedly ordinary people performing the most unordinary things. We watch, often in rapt fascination, as they do most anything from eating bugs to bungee jumping off tall bridges, always competing in a quest for prestige and usually a cash prize. Programs that would have been labeled "adult only" just a generation ago now make it as part of network broadcast television, and explicit violence has desensitized us to the mayhem of authentic violence.

I could say more about the increasingly insane things people do for entertainment, but I'd rather not!

Force

Gibbon describes the building of gigantic armaments when the real meaning is decadence. The collapse of the Soviet Union and Eastern bloc communist countries is largely attributed to the inability of those nations to keep up with the defense capability of the United States under President Reagan and the military strengthening of America in the 1980s. However, contributing to the collapse was a growing unrest within those countries as their people yearned for more freedom and self-determination. The fullness of their military could not keep up with the emptiness of their soulless system, one President Reagan rightly described as the "evil empire." For his courage and correctness, President Reagan was roundly criticized for his comment. Lest we become overly proud, we need to carefully assess our own direction, making sure that we are not guilty of believing our military strength will save us should we lose our spiritual strength.

Charles Colson, the onetime White House counsel who served time in prison for corruption before experiencing a dramatic Christian conversion, has become one of the nation's most thoughtful philosophers as well as prison reformer. Colson is on record stating, "Humanists don't understand humanity, but Christians don't understand Christianity."

The failure of many secular humanists is their assumption that people are basically victims and not responsible for their own actions, even those irrefutably evil and harmful. To be sure, there are genuinely thoughtful, sincere, well-meaning people who cling to the notion that the basic problem of humanity is a lack of education and economic equality. The obvious fallacy with this view is it does not account for why well-educated people, sometimes CEOs of major corporations, can be the worst of criminals. Highly educated and certainly economically empowered, some of the most vicious criminals are those who scheme to steal and squander the pensions of the hourly worker and individuals who gave decades of service to a company while the bosses cheated or swindled every last dime for their own indulgence.

The decadence within our country perhaps should frighten Americans as much as potential terrorists attacking our borders. When fashion is designed to call attention to a person's sexuality instead of one's face (window into personality), it's a sign that we have focused on the superficial. Pornography abounds and its harm is not nudity, which is not intrinsically offensive, but its exploitation of another human being as an object. Feminists and conservatives can actually agree that pornography reduces women to someone else's toy or plaything and fails to show respect to the personhood of each woman.

We see our addiction to consumer excess by the proliferation of products that we have come to find indispensable, such as cell phones, PDAs, iPods and MP3 players, and portable DVD players. There's nothing wrong with such modern conveniences and devices (if so, I'm a chief offender since I depend on my laptop, BlackBerry, iPod, and wristband GPS, among other "necessities," even though all of our "time-saving" devices seem to take all our time!), but it's a symptom of a society that lives on disposable items. A culture that lives by tools and toys that are disposable is susceptible to being a society that treats people as disposable, and that is the essence of true decadence.

Faith

Gibbon described faith as being marked by the decay of religion, with faith becoming form. More than anything else, I find myself grieving over what has often been empty ritual masquerading as authentic Christianity.

Neither the left nor the right has an exclusive trademark on God.

While all of us seek to invoke God's blessing, and His support for "our side," we truly miss the point. True faith leads us to take His side, and His side is not going to lower God to the puny, partisan politics we sometimes put above the very people about whom He cares most.

While I freely and unapologetically label myself "Christian" to distinguish the direction of my faith, I often choose the term "believer" or even "seeker" to better describe my own personal pilgrimage. My fear is that the term "Christian," while precious to me and dear to my very soul, is a term that is so misrepresented by those who claim it that one almost needs to place an asterisk beside it so as to footnote what it really means.

Authenticity in faith is not merely where one worships but rather how one lives. It disturbs me deeply when the term "Christian" is used as a label indicating a "better than thou" existence. I confess my own failure at being capable of fully expressing that real faith does not mean that I am better than anyone, but in fact means that I acknowledge my utter and abject spiritual poverty, my grievous sins against God and others, and my inescapable failure to live up to my own standards, much less to the perfect standards of a holy God.

To be a person of faith means I acknowledge the difference between what I am and what I need to be and know that only God's grace, through my faith in Christ, can fill that gap. I acknowledge my utter helplessness within my own strength and power to be the person I ideally would and should be. I fully recognize and willingly admit I will spend the rest of my life seeking to more fully experience true faith, hoping to practice it, but realizing my human flesh is incapable of perfecting it.

When people claim faith yet act with arrogant superiority, they defy the essence of true faith. Real faith should make us humble, mindful not so much of the faults of others but of our own faults. It should not make us more judgmental, but rather *less* judgmental, as we see others living a life with the same frailty we acknowledge within ourselves.

A true faith is one that causes us to be deeply touched by the pain of another person. Faith makes it impossible for us to ignore the cry of a child or anyone who is weak, vulnerable, or exploited. The blind bigotry of irrational racism has no place in the mind, heart, or life of a person of true faith. Few things stir my passions quite so quickly or ferociously as does racism because the ultimate manner in which to denounce and defy the heart and spirit of God is to arrogantly assert one's superiority over another. When you witness this, you witness a cover or a shield being used to compensate for one's own feeling of inferiority and insecurity. Faith is not a weapon of harm, but is practiced with a word of hope and healing.

Our nation was birthed in a spirit of faith—not a prescriptive one dictating how we were to believe, or even that we were to believe, but one acknowledging there is indeed a providence that pervades our world. While we must acknowledge it and cultivate it, it is not to be forced upon the unwilling.

The First Amendment is often used illegitimately as a way to shut out the voice of faith in the public square when it was in fact intended to do the opposite. The First Amendment declares that "Congress shall pass no law which respects the establishment" of a specific religion or prohibits the free exercise thereof. Essentially it can be defined in this simple summation: "Government is not to *prohibit* or *prefer* a particular religion or faith." It is not the government's role, responsibility, nor even its right to prohibit the expression of one's faith. Of course if that expression is a violation of the rights of others, such as those who claim their religion gives them the right to steal children, it's a different situation.

Government is not to prefer one faith over another, and it should not take a thousand lawyers to appreciate the simplicity of that principle. Those of us with deep convictions of faith know our government should guarantee that those expressions will not be prohibited. At the same time, we should be warned they will not be preferred over another in some official capacity or given special place or preference.

The First Amendment was never intended to shut out voices of faith from government, but rather intended to ensure that the voice of government did not drown out the voices of faith, the ultimate voices of conscience. The true voices of faith in America should be the voices caring for the neediest among us, those for whom no one else cares, whether they be the diseased, the criminal, the impoverished, or the insane. Indifference to the neediest among us is ultimately indifference to a God who loves equally those in the lowest positions as those in the highest.

* * *

We are a nation of laws, but we are a people rooted in deep principles of mutual respect and recognition and we have individual roles to play in the preservation of our liberty. It is our collective duty to guard our liberty against those who would destroy it either from without or within.

Largely because of my faith, I have traveled to Israel on nine different occasions. This land, holy to Christians, Jews, and Muslims, is perhaps the single most contested piece of real estate on the planet. Each time I have gone, I am not only inspired by my pilgrimages to the sites that are holy to my own Christian faith but I never fail to visit Yad Vashem, the memorial to the victims of the Holocaust.

In February 1994, my wife and I went on one of our trips and took our children with us. Our daughter, Sarah, the youngest of our three, was eleven at the time. Her brother David was thirteen and John Mark sixteen. I struggled with whether I should take Sarah to see Yad Vashem because the experience of viewing the artifacts and photographs of the horrors inflicted upon the Jewish people during Hitler's reign of terror was so intense. I was concerned it would be emotionally overpowering for her.

After Janet and I deliberated whether she should go, we decided that she should see this powerful reminder of just how cruel people can be. Our hope was that it might better explain to her why we felt compelled to leave the comfort of our peaceful and pleasant world and jump into the often savage environment of politics.

I decided I would accompany Sarah through Yad Vashem, attempting to explain the progressive manner in which Hitler and the Nazis due to their own bigotry and irrational hatred had systematically sought to annihilate the Jewish people.

Yad Vashem is presented in a chronological format, with each section of the memorial depicting the growing acts of hostility toward the Jews. In the early part of the exhibit, the yellow Stars of David that the Nazis forced to be pinned on the clothing of Jewish children were displayed. I showed Sarah how the Jewish children were isolated, targeted for ridicule and humiliation. I could tell that she was stunned by the cruelty inflicted upon children even younger than she. As we progressed through the exhibit she saw photos of Jewish children left to fend for themselves on the streets of Warsaw and other European cities after their parents were taken. She noted how the children often received their warmth from lying across the grates of a sewer, and their food from morsels tossed by sympathetic residents from their windows above.

As we gazed upon the pictures of Dachau and Auschwitz, she was introduced to the horrors of the thousands of bodies stacked on top of one another like lumber. Her grip on my hand tightened as we went through each stage of Yad Vashem. All during our visit I hoped the experience would not be overly traumatic, but powerful enough that she would never forget how important it is for people to stand up and speak out for those being victimized by evil people abusing their power.

As we approached the exit of Yad Vashem, a guest book placed by the door caught her attention. She stared at it for a moment, realizing it was there so visitors could write their names and addresses and any comments they might have about their experience. She had not said a word in quite some time, just gripped my hand more and more tightly as we walked through the experience.

At the guest book, she reached up into my pocket, took my pen, and without saying a word began to scribble her name and address. I leaned over and watched her, curious as to what she might write in the comment section. I thought perhaps what she wrote would give me an indication as to whether or not she "got it." My eleven-year-old daughter, in her childish scrawl, wrote simple words that I will never forget: "Why didn't somebody do something?"

That is all she wrote, but with those words I knew she "got it."

Without saying another word we left, boarded the bus, and for more than an hour she remained completely silent. The impact upon her was profound, but so was the impact on me as I silently prayed.

My prayer was the hope that no father will have to take his daughter through an exhibit dedicated to the memory of a country called America, once considered great, and have to try to explain why America lost its way, became indifferent, and collapsed. I prayed a father would never stand over his daughter and watch her write about America, "Why didn't somebody do something?" I knew then it would be a mission for the rest of my life.

12 Action Steps to STOP Moving the Landmarks of Liberty

1. Visit a museum of local history.
2. Take the family on an old-fashioned picnic.
3. Visit a relative in a nursing home.
4. Don't watch TV during dinner.
5. Avoid so-called reality TV shows.
6. Play checkers, chess, or cards with your family.
7. Watch the History Channel or the Biography Channel often.
8. Attend a marriage enrichment weekend sponsored by Family Life or similar organization.
9. Plan a family vacation to Washington, D.C., to see the monuments and museums of our nation's history.
10. Monitor your children's Internet activities.
11. Do some research on your family roots.
12. Ask the oldest person in your family to tell stories of his or her childhood to your children.

Chapter 11

STOP the Loss of Good Jobs and the Erosion of Agriculture

The late afternoon phone call from Jim Pickens, my director of the Department of Economic Development, delivered some of the best news that I had received as governor. Officials from Nestlé, headquartered in Switzerland and the largest food manufacturer in the world, would arrive in Little Rock the following morning and announce Jonesboro, Arkansas, as the site of a new manufacturing plant producing their Lean Cuisine line of products. Understand that anytime a governor announces almost a thousand new jobs with hundreds of millions of dollars in new investment, it is a very happy occasion and certainly cause for celebration. However, this particular announcement was especially sweet for me.

Closing the deal with Nestlé to construct a significant manufacturing plant in Arkansas was a major coup. Nestlé is not only the world's foremost producer of packaged food products it possesses a sterling reputation for their use of technology in their processes, their global marketing prowess, and equally important, their integrity as a company. Nestlé began their search for a location for this plant with an initial list of 952 communities. Over time, they narrowed the list first to 250, then to one hundred, once more down to twenty-five, and finally settled on a top ten potential site list. From there the search intensified dramatically, and ultimately the list narrowed to the final two communities under consideration: Jonesboro, Arkansas, and a site in Tennessee.

That the Nestlé plant would be a tremendous asset and boost to the economy of northeast Arkansas was well understood. What is just as important to point out is this also served as a tribute to both unified and thoughtful leadership on the part of local business officials in Jonesboro. These folks worked long, hard, and exceptionally well with those of us at the state level to carefully research the project in an effort to maximize every possible incentive and put the best possible presentation forward.

The next few hours leading up to the public announcement were quite hectic. We wanted to ensure we made just the right impression for both Nestlé and our citizens. On the morning of the announcement, we sent out employees from the Department of Economic Development to purchase a variety of products manufactured by the Nestlé Corporation so that we could provide a visual profile of the wide diversity of products Nestlé represented. Of course we wanted to specifically highlight some of the Lean Cuisine items that would now be manufactured in our state. A display consisting of a shopping cart and several tables loaded with Nestlé products was strategically positioned in the Governor's Reception Room in the State Capitol. More than once comments were overheard regarding the variety of products and familiarity with them that many of the attendees had. Officials from Jonesboro, along with Nestlé officials and representatives of state agencies involved in the process, were on hand as the big announcement commenced.

One of the main points I stressed in the announcement is key to any economic development plan. Because of the prominent place Nestlé holds within the food industry, their decision to locate in Arkansas was truly a seminal event, as they would serve as somewhat of a "bell cow" leading others to the same green pastures of opportunity to be found throughout the Natural State. Other companies would readily understand if one of the world's largest and most innovative and resourceful companies searched through 952 cites and ultimately decided that the best location was in Arkansas, there certainly was a reason for it. Clearly, this decision would add some high octane for future job recruitment.

A governor works hard for new jobs and, as a result, longs for moments such as these and savors every one of them. It is not just the opportunity to make a major press announcement of positive news. A governor understands an announcement of this magnitude is far more than a front-page news story. It means the per capita income of these workers will rise and they will possess more discretionary income and economic independence than ever before. A decision like this means fathers and mothers going to work at better jobs, bringing home to their families a larger paycheck and better benefits. They likely move closer to the American dream of home ownership and can send their children to summer camp or even to college. It means health insurance coverage for many who never had this "luxury" before. Additional dollars earned would be spent in local stores and businesses, thus substantiating the maxim "a rising tide lifts all boats."

Governors across the nation savor the announcement of a new factory, which brings such boons to their citizens. They equally dread learning that companies will be ceasing operations because of a decision to relocate those jobs to Mexico or to China, where lower labor and production costs are the norm.

The American economy has gone through many transitions in the course of our nation's history and is currently engaged in yet another significant transition. We have moved from an agrarian economy to one based on production and manufacturing, to an information and technology economy, and now to a service economy. We have managed to survive by being resilient enough to retool to meet the challenges of a changing marketplace.

It is becoming increasingly clear that the transition to a creative economy embodies a major part of the future we face. As mentioned in an earlier chapter on education, the creative economy reflects a world in which the economy is driven by taking ideas into new mediums and forms. It's not simply building a car faster or more efficiently, it's building something very different from a traditional car; it's not just making a movie but making a film with digital animation and audio that captures sight and sound never seen or heard by humans before; it's more than a new surgical procedure but one that is done robotically or by remote control with the doctor thousands of miles from the patient; it's the kind of creativity that took us from adding machines to mainframes, to PCs, to wireless handhelds or voice-activated computers. To be sure, there will remain significant sectors in our job market requiring manufacturing, service, and information, but the challenge is in providing the economic support structure necessary for the long-term viability in those sectors.

The sheer complexity of the American marketplace has made it increasingly difficult for many American companies to remain competitive with counterparts south of the border and the rapidly emerging economy of China. As do most conservatives, I believe in free trade and allowing the marketplace to push innovative ideas to the top and prices to the bottom, thus giving the consumer an opportunity to purchase items manufactured efficiently and at increasingly affordable prices. Perhaps the most compelling challenge is ensuring that a free trade correspondingly represents a fair trade.

Three dominant factors in the American economy make it increasingly difficult for jobs to remain here; excess *litigation*, excess *taxation*, and excess *regulation* combine to ultimately result in the *migration* of American jobs to marketplaces beyond our borders.

Most states, including Arkansas, have taken steps through some form of tort reform to ease the burden of potential liability, attempting to provide some relief in hopes that companies would not be forced out of business by the cost of litigation. The unfortunate fact is the cost of litigation in today's economy can often be crippling even when a company wins. Twenty-one states have enacted tort reform laws to try and stem the tide of runaway damage awards that can cause large increases in insurance premiums and business costs. When businesses project the cost parameters of their risk as a result of the courts awarding staggering damage awards (which often do more to enrich attorneys than injured citizens), decisions made to move jobs where risks are lower than the rewards become easily justified.

Excessive taxation at all levels of government has a crippling impact on job creation and retention. As is almost always the case, a few percentage points can mean the difference between profitability and failure.

Jobs and economic development encompass several areas, and in this chapter we'll focus on three specific sectors that supply jobs but are highly vulnerable to global competition—manufacturing, retail, and agriculture.

Manufacturing

While appropriate and necessary to maintain reasonable regulation for worker safety, environmental responsibility, and adequate product testing to guarantee consumer protection, some forms of regulation are virtual strangulation. Simple economic theory dictates that when the cost of compliance combined with the cost of production is equal to gross profits, financial viability is lost and, in short order, so is the industry that created the jobs.

Even as our economy sees the demand for more scientists and engineers growing at a staggering rate, the National Science Board, an independent body advising Congress and charged with overseeing the National Science Foundation, warns there is a "troubling decline" in the number of U.S. citizens seeking to become scientists or engineers. From a peak of 27,300 science and engineering doctorate degrees earned by students attending U.S. universities in 1998, we have seen graduation rates decline steadily. A recent survey by the Council of Graduate Schools reported a 32 percent decrease in applications from international students to U.S. graduate schools for a recent fall semester, which ultimately means a decrease of engineers in high-skilled jobs.

During the next ten to fifteen years, as baby boomers retire in record numbers, a job skills shortage could well be the scenario in virtually every sector of the job market. Most seriously impacted will be industries with a requirement for skilled craftspeople, technically oriented front-line workers, individuals possessing a college degree or technical education, managers, engineers, and technicians.

Currently, the United States faces a manufactured goods trade deficit that could total as much as $234 billion in deficit increase during the 2000–2006 time frame. Forty-four percent of American manufacturers surveyed in 2006 expected manufacturing to trail the overall economy. This result is up from 34 percent in the previous surveys. Basically, the survey tells us that manufacturers tended to be more pessimistic about the growth of the economy than typical economists were predicting.

My good friend John Engler, current president of the National Association of Manufacturers and an innovative former governor of Michigan, recently stated, "It is not that manufacturers are unduly pessimistic, but they are contending with unprecedented challenges that affect their outlook." According to Engler, U.S. manufacturing faces higher costs due to the rising cost of raw materials, health care, and energy. These external costs, largely beyond the control of the manufacturers, significantly lower the profitability of the companies and, according to Engler, are "tying up more funds that would otherwise be spent on investment, research and development, and new product lines."

Tony Raimondo, chairman and CEO of Behlen Manufacturing Company in Columbus, Nebraska, and a member of the National Association of Manufacturers board of directors, said that energy was one of the more challenging cost factors in his industry. Raimondo recently stated, "The government encourages us to rely more and more on natural gas for energy and then makes it virtually impossible to access more supplies of natural gas; the result is the highest natural gas prices in the world."

Engler also points to the lack of high-performance workers as another challenge identified in the survey by American manufacturers. "Half of the respondents currently have unfilled positions because they cannot find qualified workers," Engler indicated, "and 70 percent of the new jobs that survey respondents anticipate creating will be for either skilled production workers or highly educated professionals. The need for highly educated professionals specifically has nearly doubled from 2005 and we anticipate that it will continue to grow in the future."

It is becoming more and more obvious that while the challenge facing American companies to compete in the manufacturing sector is clearly tied to many components, availability of an affordable workforce remains the key. Not all is bad news to be sure. In the past few years there has been significant job growth and manufacturing has seen some rebound. At the same time, the reality of today's manufacturing environment is that plants are more sophisticated, technology-driven, and less human-labor-intensive, resulting in greater levels of productivity achieved with fewer employees.

Another piece of good news is that even medium and small companies entering the global marketplace seem to be finding emerging opportunities for their companies to expand. During a trade mission to Mexico in 2003, I met with a number of executives from Arkansas companies who, rather than lamenting the loss of manufacturing jobs to

Mexico, were celebrating new markets they located south of the border for products they were producing in Arkansas. The reality, of course, is a certain amount of transition in the types of jobs available. At the same time, we were clearly seeing more jobs created to meet the demand of the Mexican consumer than being lost to the Mexican-based manufacturer.

As my last term as governor came to an end, the Arkansas economy was experiencing the longest sustained stretch of record high revenues coupled with the lowest unemployment numbers in our history. The truth was, jobs were definitely out there to be had, but quite often these were new and different types of jobs requiring new skills and worker retraining.

A relatively new challenge in the marketplace is the growing number of Gen X workers (people born between 1964 and 1977), who enter the workforce with a different set of expectations compared to the generation before them. This latest generation of workers possesses some interesting characteristics, and I for one can't fault them for their perspective. While it would be easy to criticize them for their unwillingness to devote themselves to the "company," the truth is that the Gen X'ers are far more likely to be employed by a company who can't be expected to be very devoted to their employees either. I salute them for their restlessness and sense of urgency.

According to a study by Charlotte Shelton:

- This group as a whole isn't big on loyalty for loyalty's sake, with the average employee in his or her late twenties having already switched jobs five or six times.
- As for the time-honored process of paying one's dues in a dull job before moving up to something better, 77 percent say they would quit in a minute if offered "increased intellectual stimulation" at a different company.
- 51 percent would change jobs for the chance to telecommute.
- 61 percent of Gen X women would change jobs if they were offered more flexible hours elsewhere.
- The top three factors Gen X'ers seek in a job include positive relationships with colleagues, interesting work, and continuous

opportunities to learn. Somewhat surprisingly, recognition scored very low and power and prestige ranked dead last. Salary, a major preoccupation for baby boomers, came in third from the bottom.

• Companies willing to satisfy and keep the best Gen X employees are learning they should be "super-supportive of employees' desires to get a life outside of work." This same trend indicates that employees appreciate jobs that promote relationship building instead of a traditional corporate ladder structure.

Here, the key lesson for America seems to be a requirement to possess adaptability and resilience in a rapidly changing world, one in which the job a worker accepts today may well not exist in five to ten years. Workers should enter the marketplace expecting change, not just between companies but entire job functions, and likely repeatedly during the course of his or her lifetime.

Gone are the days when a young man could come home from military service, go to work for a company while still in his twenties, and expect to stay until he retired at age sixty-five, having worked with the same company and successfully attained secure retirement benefits.

That was my grandfather's world when he came home from serving in the Navy during World War I. He began his work career making bricks at the Hope Brickworks Company, continuing to perform his six-day-a-week job there until he retired at age sixty-five. His goal and expectation was to retire and settle into a rocking chair on his front porch, which he did until a stroke finally took its toll on his life in the late 1970s. By way of comparison, each of my three children will have worked in more jobs between college and their thirtieth birthdays than my grandfather did in his entire forty-five years in the labor market!

The classic tension between the haves and have-nots has existed and will continue to do so as long as there are people, if for no other reason than it is human nature. However, government must exercise caution in the use of its power so as to create economic opportunities designed to help everyone achieve his or her part of the American dream. The main goal should not be a simple exercise of trying to make a few people rich or keep all from poverty through artificially created income provided by the government. The focus should be directed to actual empowerment through education and employment, designed to give everyone an opportunity to provide a decent standard of living for his or her family.

There is certainly nothing at all wrong with prosperity, and no one should resent that a few people do in fact attain great levels of personal wealth. The point is, the system itself should not work solely for a few at the expense of most, but should spread the tax burden, regulatory burden, and overall risk burden. In this manner, government can perform its true mandate, making it possible for those at the lowest rungs of the economic ladder to find their way up, while those at the top rungs of the same ladder are not penalized for their productivity.

Two things critical for the government not to succumb to are penalizing productivity and subsidizing irresponsibility. In fact, quite the opposite should be our guide. Government should encourage the highest levels of productivity possible while maintaining its protective role by ensuring that consequences exist for reckless and irresponsible behavior.

Retail

Americans should never apologize for an economy based on capitalism and for providing the incentives to pursue greater levels of prosperity. Indeed, without those incentives, the spark of ambition and perseverance is severely hampered. As it is written in the Old Testament Book of Proverbs, "a worker's appetite works for him."

Success in and by others must be respected rather than resented when that success has come through hard work, innovation, and the willingness to take on high risk in order to achieve high reward. Throughout our history, there are many examples of great American companies, examples that epitomize the strength of our nation and validate the American principle of entrepreneurship.

Though often demonized because of its immense size and extraordinary growth, Arkansas-based Wal-Mart is a case study in the genius of the American marketplace. As governor of the state that Wal-Mart calls home, I often found myself in the position of defending it against uninformed and often ill-willed critics, many of whom never want the facts to get in the way of their well-planned but carelessly conducted assaults on this retailing giant.

Wal-Mart has become the largest private sector employer in approximately forty-nine of our fifty states and is rapidly becoming the largest private sector employer in many foreign nations. In fact, they reached that point in Mexico in less than ten years. While their critics have often been harsh and at times relentlessly unfair, somebody apparently likes this company, since 150 million people a week enter its doors.

Even if Wal-Mart did not have its headquarters in my home state, I could not be oblivious to the fact that this company spent almost $7 billion for merchandise and services to nearly 1,900 suppliers in Arkansas alone and at the same time helped support 67,000 jobs. In addition, this one company collected almost half a billion dollars in state and local taxes in just one year.

Labor unions in particular have sought to disparage Wal-Mart as a workplace, despite the fact that the average wage paid to its 46,000-strong Arkansas workforce is some $4.50 higher per hour than the minimum wage. In other states it seems to be an attractive place to work as well. For example, in Oakland, California, a new store with four hundred job openings was overwhelmed with 11,000 individuals applying for the positions. In Chicago, one store scheduled to employ 325 people watched as 25,000 made the effort to apply with the hopes of becoming a Wal-Mart associate.

Allow me to list three reasons for this retailing behemoth's extraordinary success and perhaps an explanation as to why it has become such an object of jealous scorn:

Wal-Mart Empowers the Consumer

The basic explanation for why Wal-Mart has been successful is it offers a variety of quality merchandise for a price the consumer is willing to pay. Having grown up in a working-class family where every dollar counted, I can assure you a store like Wal-Mart transfers purchasing power to families in the buying of their everyday necessities, resulting in the desirable effect of leaving them more discretionary income for the things they want over and above the things they simply need.

While in Mexico, an official from the Mexican Ministry of Trade explained to me the simple reason Wal-Mart was a phenomenal success in the Mexican marketplace and how it achieved the ranking as the largest private sector employer in less than a decade. He said, "Wal-Mart has empowered people in Mexico to buy the basic necessities that many could not afford before, such as shampoo, soap, and basic daily supplies."

The majority of Wal-Mart's critics, and the harshest, typically come from income levels rendering them incapable of understanding the typical Wal-Mart shopper who needs buying power in order to afford many things simply taken for granted by the affluent. This buying power enables the consumer the ability to purchase underwear, socks, or baby diapers and still have some money left for the things to be enjoyed.

An Efficient Cost Structure

Any vendor who has dealt with Wal-Mart will quickly tell you it is a company focused on driving prices lower. They will just as quickly tell you Wal-Mart is also a company willing to work with the vendor to find ways to drive production and transportation costs lower with a goal of driving the price of goods on the shelf downward rather than upward. Wal-Mart's innovative use of technology for inventory control and their distribution system is a major part of their success secret. The manner in which they track merchandise leaving the shelf is a case study in the use of innovative technology to generate price advantage. Each individual transaction entered at any store cash register is immediately uplinked to a central command center in Wal-Mart headquarters. Subsequently, items are slated for replacement utilizing the information, and then transmitted to a variety of distribution centers. When consumers purchase twenty bottles of shampoo in a store in Emporia, Kansas, on a Thursday night, by Friday morning a truck is on the way with twenty bottles of shampoo to restock the shelf. The end result is a customer not coming to purchase a popular item and finding the inventory depleted but a satisfied and repeat customer.

The logistics capability of Wal-Mart was demonstrated in an extraordinarily competent and ultimately a touchingly human manner in the direct aftermath of Hurricane Katrina. At a time when the federal government was still struggling to muster rowboats to rescue stranded people from rooftops, Wal-Mart was able to not only move truckloads of necessities to the Gulf Coast but actually opened stores and served customers almost as soon as the storms cleared the area.

As you can easily see, punishing them for their success is as ludicrous as punishing Disney World because its experience is more entertaining than the county fair, or as absurd as insisting the government put Broadway theaters out of business because they make high school plays look cheesy. America has always recognized, appreciated, and rewarded innovations resulting in benefits to the consumer. While Wal-Mart has been given an inordinate amount of blame for putting many local merchants out of business in small communities, countless others found its presence the impetus to change their business model, to survive, and yes, even thrive in the presence of a local Wal-Mart.

The argument against a company that offers more products at lower prices isn't a new or novel approach, nor one limited to Wal-Mart. It is the exact same argument made against supermarkets when they first came into existence. They were stores offering a wider variety of groceries at lower prices than the neighborhood mom-and-pop stores had offered in previous generations. History has shown numerous times and in numerous ways that it is not government but consumers who will ultimately make the decision between the intimacy of smaller stores and the lower prices and greater variety of larger stores.

An Exemplary Corporate Culture

As the chief executive of a rather large organization myself, I probably should have been unhappy with Wal-Mart as they recruited and employed a number of my top state government department heads for their corporate operations over the years. Frankly, I appreciated it when they saw the same talent and ability in those individuals as I discovered when I originally interviewed and hired them. They seek extraordinary people, treat them extraordinarily well, and in return expect extraordinary results. Far more often than not, this is exactly how things turn out.

While demonstrating extraordinary generosity in charitable giving, whether in improving education or in their many relief efforts both large and small, Wal-Mart's philanthropy is starkly juxtaposed against an almost brutally spartan corporate culture. Its headquarters and executive offices are charitably described as "functional" instead of fashionable, and executives who travel are required to stay in modest lodging, usually doubling-up in rooms to save money. There is definitely no "free lunch" at Wal-Mart, where even the top executives pay for their own coffee in the workplace. Of course, it could be argued, and Wal-Mart tends to ensure, the ultimate compensation makes it more than possible for them to afford to buy their own coffee!

There are many wonderful success stories like Wal-Mart, the majority of which started with a single visionary individual, one possessed with a strong work ethic and extraordinary integrity. Sam Walton was definitely such an individual. After losing his lease on a Ben Franklin five-and-dime store in Newport, Arkansas, Walton decided it was time to relocate to a sleepy little town called Bentonville. The move was the genesis of a most incredible American success story, one where he would open his own brand of five-and-dime stores, learning and studying and finally deciding he could improve upon them by creating and implementing what became the Wal-Mart model.

Another Arkansas-based international giant, Tyson Foods, got its start when the grandfather of current chairman John Tyson sold eggs from the back of his pickup truck to local residents in Springdale, Arkansas. From the back of that little egg truck grew the world's largest producer of protein, selling eggs, poultry, beef, and pork. Today, Tyson Foods operates with the admirable but simple mission statement espousing they "are a company of people engaged in the production of food, seeking to pursue truth and integrity, and committed to creating value for our shareholders, our customers, and our people in the process."

Stephen's Inc. is yet another Arkansas-based company with an incredible story. Founders Witt and Jack Stephens got their start by selling bonds, eventually developing a financial empire widely recognized as the largest investment bank off Wall Street. Their vision, experience, and willingness to accept risk resulted in the financing of many a start-up company and they capitalized on enormous opportunities for entrepreneurs throughout the world. You can be assured both Jack and Witt, and the company that continues today, looked for traits similar to their own as they worked in the economy-creation business. Yet the extraordinary wealth obtained by the Stephens family is mirrored by the equally extraordinary amount of money they return through giving to charitable causes. Literally hundreds of millions of dollars have been turned back to improve health care, education, and infrastructure, in turn touching in a positive way literally thousands of lives.

These wonderful success stories serve as a reminder that our nation needs to rekindle the entrepreneurial spirit. We need to create a marketplace where ideas are encouraged, where innovation is rewarded, and where investment in ideas is supported, in order to create jobs and wealth. Government's role must be to facilitate rather than complicate this entrepreneurial spirit, and government should seek to empower rather than imperil or impede the possibilities that risk takers generate each and every day.

Agriculture

There are two essential requirements a nation should be able to provide its citizens—freedom and security. To accomplish them, a nation must have the ability to defend itself and the ability to feed itself.

Americans today take for granted they will be able to obtain good food at low prices. Anyone failing to comprehend or fully appreciate the dramatically low price of food in the United States is definitely a person with little experience in international traveling. We should find it exceptionally frightening when a lack of understanding of the American agriculture process results in government policies that threaten the very heart of our farm economy.

The American farmer not only feeds American families but a substantial portion of the rest of the world's population, both human and animal. A significant amount of the wheat, soy beans, rice, cotton, and corn for grain produced in the United States finds its way through exports to Asia, Western Europe, and Latin America. America would export even more of our agricultural production if the marketplaces of the world were as open to the American farmer as our marketplace is to the rest of the world.

Of growing concern is that without some change of policies our country may well run out of farmers because their median age is currently fifty-nine years old. Due to the extraordinary risk involved in making a success of farming, coupled with the dramatically high cost of starting or fully capitalizing a farm, many younger Americans are increasingly unwilling to enter or remain in farming. Compounding the problem are continual fears created by onerous government regulations and rapid policy changes, which often have a dramatic and negative impact on the potential for profitability.

There appears to be some lack of appreciation for the value of our farmers and their contributions not only to our tables but to our overall economy. In 2006, an American family of four spent on average $4,200 on food for the year, about 9.5 percent of their family budget. Breaking it down a little further, we find 5.4 percent of those food dollars was spent on food prepared and eaten at home, and the remaining 4.1 percent went to eating outside the home.

What makes these figures extraordinary is that they are far lower in every category than the amount any other developed nation on earth spends for food. A glance at figures for the United Kingdom shows the average family spending 22 percent of their income on food, while Germany and Australia are close with 21 percent. In New Zealand, 20 percent of the budget is spent on food and in France 18 percent.

Families in these developed nations are still spending nearly twice that of the American family. This is a huge economic advantage to America. Since Americans spend such a smaller portion of their total budget on food, an enormous amount of their income is freed up to provide them the power to purchase other goods and services. This directly leads to a much broader and more diverse economy, in turn creating more jobs and greater insulation against sudden sharp downturns in the economy.

Those who do not fully appreciate the low cost of American food are probably the same people who disparage the subsidies that exist for farming operations. Certainly the process of subsidizing certain commodities needs to be examined on a regular basis to ensure the process is responsible and reasonable, but they are still a critical part of our economy.

It has been the policy of the United States to subsidize certain farm products by paying farmers a stipend for their crops to ensure the farmers will receive a guaranteed minimum price. To some this is controversial and some conservatives believe that all agricultural subsidies should be discontinued and allow the market to function. In an ideal world, this would be a good practice, but American farmers are competing with highly subsidized farmers in Europe and Asia, and the fixed costs faced by the farmers involving land, equipment, seed, and supplies means that even if they don't produce a single stalk of corn, they are going to have some significant expenses.

Keeping the American farmer in business is not just good for the farmer but for the consumer. The theory and subsequent policy behind subsidies is that production is maintained at a higher level, driving food costs lower. This not only enables families to keep from starving (obviously a very important aspect!) but, as previously stated, it empowers them as consumers and generates stability in the farming economy so that America remains a producing rather than consuming nation.

We all have experienced the disastrous consequences of being dependent upon foreign sources of oil for our energy needs. Imagine the further weakening of America if we were also dependent on foreign sources for our food needs. Ensuring that America feeds herself is not only a matter of good economic and agricultural policy, it is perhaps equally as important as good security policy.

Farm subsidies also help insulate farmers from circumstances well beyond the marketplace, factors they can't control such as natural disasters, including droughts, floods, hurricanes, or tornadoes, and even sudden spikes in the cost of fuel, feed, and fertilizer. Our farmers carry huge debt loads for equipment and investment and the risk each year can be dramatic, often burdensome. Maintaining a strong national farm policy designed to help protect farmers from going under due to circumstances beyond their control is what helps stabilize low food prices and what helps keep the rest of the American economy vibrant.

Here in Arkansas, we have a strong agricultural economy with 165 different crops grown in the state on some 47,000 farms averaging 306 acres in size. Arkansas ranks number one in rice production, number two in broiler and other meat-type poultry production, number two in egg production, and can be found consistently in the top two or three in a number of categories of vegetable or farm crop production. Over the years, I have watched as our farmers struggled to endure the challenges of fluctuating prices, policies, and natural perils and never fail to find myself amazed they are willing to go back year after year.

It is my hope our nation's policies in agriculture will always be mindful that a nation that can not only feed itself but do so with relatively inexpensive cost is a nation strong, but a nation hungry or one dependent on foreign governments for its food is a nation already on its knees.

Our nation continues to benefit from people with simple dreams. These are individuals willing to risk all for the opportunities they believed would come to someone with the courage and vision to take great risk for the hope of great rewards.

I would like to introduce you to one such person. In March 1998, I began to notice a young black male, dressed in a sweatshirt with a hood pulled over his head, appearing to sell something on a street corner just one block from the State Capitol. I would see him as I made my way to work each day. Some might mistakenly assume he was either panhandling or, even worse, selling drugs, but they would be quite wrong. I found out this young man, whose name is Chris, stood on that corner every day from seven to nine in the morning. He picked a busy intersection so that business would be brisk, locating where the exit ramp of Interstate 630 meets Martin Luther King, Jr. Drive, adjacent to the State Capitol. He sold fruit to drivers who were passing by. His offering was a plastic bag containing a banana, an apple, and an orange for one dollar. Chris would make about $30 each morning. He was always there. Though he certainly demonstrated an impressive work ethic, equally impressive was the smile he had on his face for everyone who passed by. The reason for the hood over his head was simple: It was cold outside!

Chris was well aware he could make more money in one drug deal than he did spending hours on that street. He knew because he had tried that before and in fact had been sentenced to prison for selling drugs. Fortunately, Chris was accepted to a correctional boot camp as an alternative to full-time incarceration, and after completing his incarceration, he took a job in a manufacturing facility. With a full-time job already in hand, why did he take on the added role of selling fruit? Because a faith experience led him to change his perspective on life and desire not just to exist but to exceed the expectations that others had for him. Chris's goals were to one day have his own produce stand, and eventually his own health food store. Yes indeed, all of this would be quite a journey for someone who was once headed to prison. But Chris was now headed in a different direction, to a career and a kind of pinnacle of personal success.

12 Action Steps to STOP
the Loss of Good Jobs and the
Erosion of Agriculture

1. Be computer literate and current.

2. Read a bestselling business book every three months.

3. Visit or volunteer in a job training program.

4. Tutor an adult in a literacy program.

5. Talk to local business owners about their challenges to attract and keep employees.

6. Purchase fresh produce often, especially if you have a local farmers' market.

7. Try to find and enjoy organic or natural foods and grass-fed beef raised on a self-sustaining farm.

8. Mentor a student in an after-school program.

9. Tour a manufacturing plant in your area.

10. When possible, purchase food and durable goods made in the USA.

11. Contribute to a scholarship for a student to attend college.

12. Take a course at your community college.

Chapter 12

STOP BEING A SELFISH CITIZEN

The galleries are full of critics that play no ball, fight no fights, and they make no mistakes because they attempt nothing. Down in the arena are the doers, they make mistakes because they attempt many things. The man who makes no mistakes lacks the boldness and spirit of adventure. He is the one who never tries anything, he is the brake on the wheel of progress, and yet it cannot be said that he truly makes no mistakes because the biggest mistake that he makes is the fact that he tries nothing and does nothing except to criticize someone who does do things.

—THEODORE ROOSEVELT

Theodore Roosevelt reminds us that the easiest work of all is the work of criticizing the real work that others do. America needs to be restored to its greatness where it faithfully and responsibly serves its own citizens and is also a respected beacon of hope and opportunity for the rest of the world.

It will require more than the shouting matches on the cable networks; more than clever monologues on talk radio; more than hours of phoned-in hysteria or blogs of emotional and irrational ravings from people with more time on their hands than information in their heads. Neither will America's greatness be discovered inside the circle known as the Washington Beltway.

America's greatness will be around the dinner table where families gather each evening; it is in the pews of churches and synagogues and other houses of worship where people seek to focus on something larger than themselves; it is on the sidelines of a Little League baseball game where an adult brings encouragement to young, aspiring athletes and is not paid a dime for his efforts; it is beside a country pond where a mom helps a six-year-old bait a hook and teaches the lessons of patience while waiting on the cork to go underwater.

In this chapter, I want to explore how we can cease being selfish citizens, consumed only with our own prosperity, security, and needs. We will explore ways of becoming citizens whose actions can truly help restore America's greatness. We will examine this in two parts; the first deals with preparing individually, the second focuses on key steps to taking these personal values to the public arena.

Personal Preparation for Unselfish Citizenship

Too many of us are like the man at the end of a day's work who parks his German car, goes inside to sip Chinese tea, turns on his Japanese-made television, slips off his Italian loafers, takes a French-made pen, and writes on his Canadian-milled paper a letter to his congressman complaining about all the money that is leaving the United States! Everyone wants to eat from a clean plate but someone has to do the dishes!

Rarely do I find an American citizen who is completely and totally satisfied with the way things are. Most every citizen believes we could do better in some area, whether it is providing better border security, doing a better job in developing alternative fuels, making health care more available and affordable to our citizens, or making education more effective for the children of our nation.

I often hear people say, "*They* ought to do something about improving our roads, *they* ought to do something about lowering our taxes, *they* ought to do something about drug use, *they* ought to do something about the rising cost of health care."

If you have ever wondered why *they* didn't do a better job, maybe it's because it never occurred to you that *they* rarely do anything. Life changes when *they* get fired and *we* take their place.

America certainly needs new leadership, but not just new leaders at the top who run for public office (though frankly that is a starting place). We need leaders in every state, county, community, neighborhood, street, and family.

Leaders recognize there is a certain amount of pulling required to move things. Pulling goes against gravity and is not always comfortable, but it is necessary to create tension that stresses and stretches us. Leadership is a sacred trust that is on loan from the people. The leader does not own it, but is simply entrusted with it and must be responsible for it. As I have often said to my own staff, "we lead by loving not by shoving."

True leaders do not find it necessary to constantly announce that they are in charge, because people are more than willing to give the reins of leadership to one who models leadership. Leadership means getting in front and asking others to join rather than getting behind, kicking people from the rear, and telling them what they should be doing.

Here are seven key elements to being personally prepared for leadership:

Dream Your Purpose

Don't be like the little boy with the gun flung over his shoulder out in the woods hunting. When a man approached him and asked, "Son, what are you hunting for?" the little boy replied, "I don't know. I haven't found it yet." Leadership begins with a vision; a goal; a true dream that is definite, definable, and doable.

A lighthearted but hilarious comedy starring Sandra Bullock called *Miss Congeniality* featured a scene in which beauty pageant contestants were to discuss their "platform" of what they would like to achieve. Their stock answer was "world peace." With no disrespect to pageant winners, I'm not sure we end global conflict by electing a particular twenty-one-year-old beauty to wear a crown based on her ability to sing, dance, walk gracefully in an evening gown, and look stunning in a swimsuit!

Ask yourself, "What is my personal vision, dream, or goal?" Do you want to see a new playground for your child's school; do you want to have a local park cleaned up so that people can enjoy it; do you truly aspire to see more money spent on adequate housing and food for the poor; or do you want a tax policy that encourages venture capital to be made available to would-be entrepreneurs? As you dream *your* purpose, define what really is important to you and what really makes your clock tick so you will know the course necessary to help make it happen.

Determine Priorities

One reason that many people who dream dreams never see them fulfilled is because they never learn to separate the urgent from the important. One of my most challenging concerns has always been separating those things that someone else had determined to need my immediate attention and those things that are really important enough to actually do this moment.

I have learned that it is important to write out daily to-do lists because there is truth in the saying, "The palest of ink is still better than the sharpest memory."

When I was in the ninth grade, I was fortunate enough to have a Student Council advisor, Mrs. Anna E. Williams, who saw potential in me. She knew that I needed more direction and discipline to fully realize my potential. From the ninth through the twelfth grades (when I eventually served as the president of Hope High School student body), she required me to report to her classroom thirty minutes before school each day. I was to present to her a list of the things that I intended to accomplish that day and show her the list from the day before with a line through those items which I had accomplished and which were not required to be a carryover.

This habit was so ingrained in me that to this day I am still a compulsive list maker and often will have several different lists in my pocket with daily, weekly, or long-term goals on each. My wife and children are quick to remind me that it is really not necessary for me to make a list for them each day as well!

I strongly believe that people who get things done are people who have defined exactly what they wish to get done and are constantly working toward definite and determined goals.

One way to stay on track toward goals and make sure that the priorities are kept is to not waste time deciding more than once about what can be best defined as duty. I learned early in life that once a decision had been made about a specific responsibility, it was a complete waste of time and energy to go back and revisit that decision each and every time action was required.

For example, if you decide in August to enroll in a class that meets three times a week for sixteen weeks, then you should never wake up and ask, "Am I going to class today?" Of course you are! You made that decision in August, so don't waste time deciding on that three times a week for the next sixteen weeks. If you join a church, you have made a decision to attend that church faithfully and give it your support. Don't insult your own integrity by getting up each Sunday and asking whether you will go to church that day! If the average American paid his or her bills like we pay out our obligations to memberships in clubs, to churches, or to our civic duty, we would all have judgments filed against us for nonpayment!

Learn to make the "have to's" in your life the "want to's" in your life. Determine priorities by those things that really interest you. Learn to do a few things well or you will end up doing everything with mediocrity.

Demand Planning

As a young child I attended the Garrett Memorial Baptist Church in Hope, Arkansas. In our Sunday school classroom there was a little sign on the wall with six simple words: "Plan Your Work, Work Your Plan." I saw those words every Sunday. At age six, that didn't make much sense, but by the time I was sixteen it became one of the most important principles I knew to apply to my everyday life.

If we fail to plan, we truly plan to fail.

People who build great architectural wonders follow extensive and exquisitely detailed plans. Just imagine the disaster if a construction crew attempted to build a skyscraper without plans, simply coming to work each day saying, "We will just work real hard and try our best to make all the pieces fit."

Just as making a list is important to determine *what* to do, developing a plan gives us a blueprint for *how* to do it. I am convinced that no one is ready to do great things until they have planned *how* they will accomplish those things.

Develop People

If I have had any genuine success in my life it is not due to innate greatness or talent within me but the fact that I recognized my many weaknesses and tried to build a team of people around me who were good at
the things in which I struggled.

One of the most profound truths about marriage was uttered by that
famous American theologian Rocky Balboa in the movie *Rocky*. In a conversation Rocky was having with Paulie, the brother of his future wife,
Adrian, Paulie asks Rocky what he saw in her. Rocky uttered one word,
"Gaps." After a pause he explained, "We fill each other's gaps." I am not
sure Sylvester Stallone, who wrote the script, intended to be so profound,
but his answer couldn't have been more dead center of the bull's-eye.

Great marriages don't happen because two equally gifted people, neither with a single flaw, are able to join their strengths. Great marriages
happen when people are able to see their own weaknesses and allow a
spouse to "fill the gaps." What is true in a marriage is true for a business,
athletic team, political movement, or any organization.

The single most important job a leader has is to make other people
successful. It has been my own experience that if I will focus on making
the people around me successful they will in turn make me successful.
Learn that it is always best to remember that people are working *with*
you, not *for* you.

In the very first week I took office as governor I made a speech to our
staff and told them that I was going to be placing a photograph with an
inscription that read "Our Boss" in the outer office and wanted them to
make sure they took a look at it from time to time. I am sure that when
I first announced this some might have thought me filled with extraordinary ego, intending to place my likeness in the frame.

However, I told them that while the inscription would indeed say
"Our Boss" *my* photograph would never be in that frame. I announced
that we would change the photo every couple of weeks and that it would
be a picture of some ordinary Arkansas citizen so that we would be reminded who the boss *really* is. It is *not* the guy in the corner office with
the title after his name. It's not that guy people line up in the lobby to
see in ten- or fifteen-minute intervals. The real boss for whom we all
work is any one of the 2.7 million citizens in our state, whether it is an

elderly couple celebrating their golden wedding anniversary; a young, single mom trying to balance a job, two kids, and night school; or an eleven-year-old proudly holding up the blue ribbon that he earned at the state fair. I have always insisted that we treat everyone with dignity and respect, whether the richest person in our state or a homeless person simply coming in to get out of the cold.

In developing people, keep in mind that leaders should never ask others to do what the leader is unwilling to do. Nothing is more discouraging to people in any organization than to be assigned a task by those who make it clear that such a task would be beneath them.

Leaders understandably sometimes have to ask others to do things that may not be pleasant or that the leader may not be able to join in doing. Yet it's more an attitude than an action on the part of the leader, making sure to think through the things that are being asked of others and never forgetting that every task is important. In an orchestra the piccolo may not be the largest or the loudest instrument, but when called for in the symphony, its role is vital.

Delegate Power

The least effective leader is the one who seeks to do everything himself. Good leaders delegate the power to others and by so doing they work smarter and not just harder.

Some leaders make the mistake of delegating the *responsibility* but failing to delegate the *authority and power* to actually accomplish what's being required. Don't simply give *orders*, but rather give *freedom* for people to carry out the instructions. Good leaders clearly define the goals and allow there to be freedom in how those goals are reached. Delegating also means that as surely as you give people the freedom to succeed you also empower them with the freedom to fail. One cannot be granted without the other, so make sure that when the mission is defined, not only communicate what should be done but also how well it should be done, and when it should be completed.

Deliver Praise

People like to be recognized for a job well done. Period. Sometimes no amount of money can pay quite like a simple "thank you." If you don't have time to say thank you at the end of a task completed, then consider that you didn't have time to assign the task in the first place.

Remember that even with children the promise of ice cream works better than the threat of a spanking. Of course if you read my previous book, *Quit Digging Your Grave with a Knife and Fork* (and I sure hope you have!), you know that it might be better to reward a child with something other than food, but you get the point. While there are many ways to reward those around you for a job well done, no reward will be complete without a sincere, cheerful word of appreciation. People will jump through fire when they know it will be appreciated, but people wouldn't walk across the street if they believe it will be taken for granted.

Display Perseverance

Our daughter-in-law, Lauren, has a tiny little toy shih tzu dog named Skittles. My wife fell in love with the dog and started asking me to get her one "like Skittles." Because we have had a big eighty-pound Labrador retriever, Jet, for eight years, the thought of bringing a tiny dog into the house to share space with a well-established "only child" of a dog seemed like a bad idea.

Months of her dropping hints and outright pleading finally took their toll. For Christmas 2005 I gave Janet her own little toy shih tzu, who at seven weeks old weighed only a pound and a half. She had already told me that if she got a puppy she would name him Sonic because of her affinity for the Sonic drive-in restaurants where she is a regular customer, alternating between cherry limeades and vanilla root beer. I presented Sonic at our staff Christmas party, and brought the little puppy to her in a forty-four-ounce Sonic soft drink cup. He fit quite comfortably!

The next few months were quite interesting as we watched our well-trained, well-bred, and well-behaved Lab try to figure out what to do with this tiny little creature that he surely thought must have been something other than a dog. Whatever indifference Jet may have shown the little interloper, it didn't deter Sonic one bit.

From day one Sonic acted as if he, too, were a big dog and whatever Jet did, Sonic tried to do also. Sometimes Sonic would even challenge Jet for a bowl of food or a toy. Jet, being ever the typical, docile, easy-to-please Lab, would often simply walk away rather than engage in a fight with a dog a fraction of the size of the ducks he retrieved during hunting season.

As I watched the dogs learn to get along and establish their own space, I was reminded of a truth I had heard years before: "It is not the size of the dog in the fight, but the size of the fight in the dog that determines the outcome."

A quality absolutely necessary for leaders to lead and ultimately to win is to display perseverance. The only certain way to lose is to quit before the end of the game. One of the most inspirational speeches I ever heard was given by Clebe McLary, a Marine who had been severely wounded in Vietnam, losing both legs, one arm, and his sight in one eye. It was miracle enough that he was alive, but a greater miracle was his unquenchable spirit and optimism. I will never forget one statement he made: "I have never lost at anything. Sometimes the game ended before I finished playing, but I never lost at anything."

Taking It to the Streets!

Once a person has come to grips with the important internal battles and settled within one's soul principles to personally live by, it's time to leave the practice field and get in the game!

A salesman came to a farmer's house and started his pitch, attempting to sell seed to the farmer. A few minutes into his delivery he was taken aback by the sight of something strange in the farmer's yard. It was a pig with a wooden leg. The salesman couldn't help but ask, "I've never seen that before. Why does your pig have a wooden leg?"

"That is no ordinary pig," said the farmer. "Why that is probably one of the smartest pigs in the world. I was out on my tractor one day plowing when the tractor turned over on me and had me pinned. The pig came running to my rescue, dug a hole out from under me giving me enough space to crawl out from under the tractor, which saved my life."

"Well that is a wonderful story," said the salesman, "but it doesn't explain why the pig has a wooden leg."

"Well, that pig is not just any old pig," said the farmer. "Late one night when we were all asleep a fire started in our house. We would have slept right through it and probably all died, but the pig smelled the smoke and began snorting and oinking so loudly that he woke us all up and we were able to get out of the house before it burned. Why that pig saved the lives of my entire family!"

By this time exasperated, the salesman said, "Sir, it is obvious that your pig is a remarkable animal and probably more amazing than Lassie, but you still have not explained why your pig has a wooden leg."

"Mister, you don't think we would be stupid enough to eat a pig that smart all at one time, do you?" said the farmer.

If you join me in feeling that our nation has lost some of its greatness, not only in terms of how we perceive ourselves but how others see us, then surely you understand that we didn't get there all at once. One of the most important lessons in engaging in the world of public service and in the field of public policy is to realize that the changes in our culture we don't like were incremental, and the changes we want to see happen are also going to be incremental. If you don't have the patience or the perseverance to go the distance, it is best not to even enter the contest.

Worthwhile battles in the political arena are not for the easily discouraged or the faint of heart. Politics can be a full-contact sport. While it shouldn't be and doesn't have to be dirty, one cannot be guaranteed that others will always fight fair. If you can't handle being fouled, then it would be better to buy a ticket and watch from the stands. If you can't stand the sight of your own blood, your role might need to be limited to helping others and not actually putting your name on the ballot and your neck on the line.

Let me list five key things that will help us successfully cross the finish line:

Stand by Your Convictions

Too many so-called leaders don't really know what they stand for other than they stand for themselves to be reelected. There ought to be some issues that you believe in so strongly that you would rather lose an election than lose your self-respect by walking away from the very thing that got you in this process to begin with.

I have often said that there are two kinds of leaders, *thermometers* and *thermostats*. A thermometer can read the temperature of the room and accurately report what the temperature is. Some politicians are like thermometers. They conduct clever opinion polls and then take positions that reflect and mirror the temperature of the people they have polled. That is *thermometer leadership* and it is *not* what America needs.

Thermostat leadership is dramatically different. A thermostat can certainly read the temperature and report what it is, but its sole purpose for existence is to adjust the temperature to what it should be, not merely to read it as it is. *Thermostat leadership* is aware of poll numbers and perceptions but is even more aware of the principles that are worth living for and, if necessary, dying for. There are most likely core convictions that are so important to you that they represent lines that you are unable or unwilling to cross. If there is nothing that you believe in that strongly, you probably enjoy being an observer rather than a combatant.

Above all else, remember that there is a big difference between a person's *values* and recognizing the *true "value" of every person*. Many political debates center around whose *"values"* are superior as they relate to the family, the economy, education, health care, and so on. I am convinced that even those of us who are conservatives have really missed that the true issue is not creating a must believe set of values but rather adhering steadfastly to the notion that every person intrinsically *has* value and that the worth of each human being should drive our public policies.

A person who sees his or her own value will in fact have values. The reason a person throws himself or herself away with drugs, alcohol, promiscuity, or some other form of vagrant behavior is because that person has ultimately rejected his or her own value.

Support Candidates

If you decide not to be a candidate, then you should decide to fervently and faithfully support those who share your core convictions and who are likely to act on your behalf if elected. Support means more than voting for, although it won't help much if you don't vote. Don't expect to find perfect candidates because there aren't any! Judge more by a candidate's spirit than his or her speeches.

Before I got into politics, I helped raise millions of dollars for various church, nonprofit, and education-related causes, most of which were faith-based. When I first ran for office and started raising political money, I came to realize that there were many similarities between raising money for church projects and political causes, but there was one major distinction. I often said and truly believed that in church "God loves a cheerful giver." I came to learn in politics you are willing to take from a grouch!

Give generously and sacrificially to candidates you want to see elected. Write the largest possible check that you can and remember that if this person were unwilling to run for office it might be left up to you to do it. If *you* had run for office you would have given up your evenings, your weekends, and your privacy—even if you didn't win! You probably would lose income and you would have to ask people to help pay for printing materials, media advertising, staff, and supplies. If you aren't the candidate, try to give to that candidate the same amount you would have hoped someone would have given had you run.

Not only do you need to write a big check, but you need to commit a big chunk of your personal time to helping the candidate, whether operating phone banks, helping to do advance work for an event, raising money, or hammering yard signs.

People ask me how I was able to overcome all odds and be elected lieutenant governor in 1993 despite being greatly outspent by my opponent and having none of the traditional insiders supporting me. Running as a Republican in a state that was overwhelmingly Democrat (and that had just jubilantly sent one of their own to the White House) was tough. I tell them that it was not so much *my* victory but the victory of people across the state who, as conservatives and as Republicans, wanted to win and were willing to work hard for it to happen.

One of the true matriarchs of the Arkansas Republican Party was a precious and dear Christian lady, the late Ada Mills of Clarksville, Arkansas. Ada had been a staunch Republican her entire adult life and faithfully supported the GOP candidates in Arkansas even when it was utterly futile to do so. Miss Ada was the epitome of perseverance and patience.

When I ran for lieutenant governor in July 1993, I felt I might actually win the day I got a phone call from a supporter in Johnson County. The voice on the other end told me that Miss Ada was spotted in a vacant field across from the Wal-Mart store in Clarksville on a sweltering hot July afternoon with several of my yard signs. This eighty-three-year-old woman was out pounding them into the hard ground trying to make sure I got elected!

I am not where I am today because I was the greatest candidate or because I had all the answers to all the questions. I am where I am today only because extraordinary people believed in an ordinary candidate who was willing to articulate shared beliefs. Whatever victory was attributed to me was truly the result of people on whose shoulders I was carried.

Strive for Coalitions

Sometimes it seems that the Republican Party is the only army that shoots its wounded! At other times we form a firing squad by creating a circle. Many of the defeats Republican candidates or causes have suffered have not been due to the effectiveness of the message or machine of the Democratic Party but because of petty divisions within the GOP.

Ronald Reagan encouraged Republicans to remember the "Eleventh Commandment for Republicans": "Thou shall not speak ill of another Republican." Some Republicans break that commandment and several of the original ten on top of it!

Both within the party and sometimes from independent issue-focused political groups, I have seen the attitude of those who demand all or nothing and they demand it now or never. That kind of approach usually yields *nothing* and yields it *forever*.

While we should never compromise our core values, we do have to win the battle in increments. The timetable to do *everything* starts with a time to do *something*. Moving the ball downfield and positioning for the touchdown is better than being held at the line of scrimmage, or worse, being pushed back behind where we started. Yet through the years I have seen some groups and individuals who actually pride themselves on how unpopular they are and how ineffective they have become, virtually boasting of being pushed back at every attempt to pass any legislation or accomplish one single thing. Instead of being a badge of honor it should be a scar of shame, for who of us wants to spend time, money, and effort only to be proud we have consistently lost every battle? That doesn't prove that we were right, only that we didn't know how to play the game very well! I didn't enter politics because I enjoyed the battle, but because I really wanted to see a nation that better reflected the inherent goodness and decency that I saw. And I never expected things would go all my way. From the first day I walked through the doors, I never assumed that the opposition would simply give up and quit because a handful of folks like me showed up to challenge the status quo.

Getting things done in the political arena often involves creating coalitions that today may appear to be made up of unlikely partners. There is an important lesson: "He who is my opponent today may be my friend tomorrow." On any given issue, that can be exactly right. Never burn bridges and end relationships. The very people that we are disgusted with today may be the ones whose votes tomorrow help win an important battle.

Just as husbands and wives don't always agree, neither do people within the same political party. We should build around the agreements rather than focus on the disagreements. If you do find yourself at odds with the leaders of your own party, then for heaven's sakes take it to *them*, and to them alone, not to others or, worse, to the general public! You don't have to agree with everything members of your party might say or do, but you can't show support if you publicly question every position your colleagues take. And this is a principle that works for business or marriage as well as for politics.

We should strive for *unity* but not expect *union*. For those who don't understand the difference, let me illustrate. Taking two tomcats, tying their tails together, and tossing them over a clothesline is *union*, but it is most certainly not *unity*. Unity is more akin to a married couple who might not agree on everything, but remain committed to their marriage because they realize that the marriage is actually more important than who gets to hold the TV remote. (And for those who aren't sure, it's the husband who is supposed to hold it.) Being able to get along and work together in a civil manner is the goal.

Solve Crises

The ultimate reason to get involved in any political endeavor and the ultimate purpose for the existence of political parties and their efforts to elect candidates is to solve real problems and repair things that are broken. I learned as a governor that hard-core Democrats would be willing to vote for me if I could improve our highways, health care system, schools, and environment, and make government more efficient for the people who have to deal with it.

For as long as I have been an Arkansas driver, I hated the process in our state of getting a car tag. It was a tedious process that involved going to one's insurance agent for a piece of paper indicating insured status, going to the county assessor's office and documenting having assessed personal property, then making a trip to the county treasurer's office to obtain a piece of paper proving payment of personal property taxes. Then one had to get another piece of paper from the revenue office describing the registration renewal date for an automobile, and then go to one of the several licensed car inspectors and get yet *another* piece of paper proving that we could honk our horn and that our blinkers worked.

After all of those papers had been collected—in order—we were able to go to the revenue office in person and take a number and get in line to inch our way to the desk and present our stack of papers to obtain a tiny little decal to go on the back of our license plate. That sticker would last for a year. If, God forbid, we didn't have one of the pieces of paper with us or it had not been filled out properly, we left the line to go and start all over again. I often said that anyone who could ever simplify the car tag process in Arkansas could be elected for life!

When I became governor, one of the first things I did was insist that the senior staff in our office and all of our agency heads be required to spend half a day each month working alongside a state employee in some level of state government. They were prohibited from going to work in an office at the executive level; they had to be out where basic state government services were being performed. During my tenure I personally did everything from mow the grounds at state parks, serve as an intake clerk at a Department of Human Services desk (taking applications for food stamps), change adult diapers at a human development center for severely disabled adults, and follow a world-renowned oncologist during rounds at our world-class University of Arkansas Medical Science campus. The first thing I did, however, was spend a day with front-line revenue office workers at the Marion, Arkansas, location near West Memphis. The employees there had been doing that work for an average of fifteen years. I asked them, "If you were king for a day and could change the process of getting a car tag to make it simple, what would you do?"

I then listened and took notes. What I learned from them became the basis for how we turned one of the most complicated processes for our citizens into one of the simplest. It can now be done by phone, mail, or Internet in less than three minutes, unless a person just insists on going to the revenue office. Even then it's a streamlined process. I discovered people were less concerned that I was a Republican and more grateful for the fact that we had made the car registration system simple.

That was the same experience I had when we took what had been deemed by *Trucker* magazine as the "worst interstate highway system in the country" and turned it into one of the best, and when the ARKids First health program led the nation in reducing the number of uninsured children. People are less concerned by ideologies and political affiliations than they are by whether or not we can get the job done.

Sacrifice Comfort

Throughout these chapters I have probably not painted too rosy a picture of getting involved in political endeavors. I wanted to paint a realistic picture of the pain and perils of the process. To be effective one needs to expect not just a slight heartburn but true heartache. People you thought were your friends will abandon you, and people you knew were your enemies will prove it! While some people will accuse you of breaking your promises to them, other people will break their promises to *you*.

People will often tell me that they are behind me, but what that means is that they are *way* behind me and nowhere near where the bullets are flying. While occasionally a corrupt politician, like Randy Duke Cunningham of San Diego, will sell his office for personal wealth, more often than not people in public service will sacrifice their level of income compared to what they could have made had they used the same talents in the private sector.

During my tenure I had the distinction of being the lowest-paid governor in America, but of course I reminded people they got what they paid for! If I ever tried to complain, my wife reminded me, "You asked for this job." And I did! I didn't ask for it when I first got it, as it was thrust upon me unexpectedly, but I did ask for it after that, not once, but twice.

The wonderful people of Arkansas gave me the greatest joy and privilege I could have ever imagined serving as their governor for ten and a half years. I still am awed by the fact that a kid coming out of the humble and challenging circumstances I did could end up living in the Governor's Mansion, traveling around the world, and being able to give leadership to a state and help influence a nation. It is especially amazing when I think back to that same person at age eight taken by his father to shake the hand of a governor because, "You may live your whole life and never meet the governor."

Perhaps there is yet another chapter of my life yet to be lived in public service. It is one of the important, yet most difficult decisions that I face, but this much I do know—should I choose to again enter the arena and engage in a battle, I will do so because I still think that it really matters for people to go from Hope to Higher Ground!

12 Action Steps to STOP
Being a Selfish Citizen

1. Pray before meals.

2. Make a to-do list every day.

3. Attend church, synagogue, or house of worship at least once a week.

4. Write a thank-you note to someone each day.

5. When attending a banquet, go out of your way to thank your server.

6. Read a chapter in the Book of Proverbs each day.

7. Call people by name.

8. Write a note to a public official—ask for nothing, but thank him or her for one specific thing.

9. Help a total stranger carry a heavy item to his or her car.

10. Buy Girl Scout cookies.

11. Rake the leaves in a neighbor's yard.

12. Call an old friend from high school to catch up.

CONCLUSION

The greatest danger any of us face is not a calamity itself but the willful acceptance of it as inevitable and unchangeable. Our tribulations can actually make us stronger, but the moment we stop growing from them and going beyond them, we begin our descent into despair and the acceptance of a life of limited capacity.

Greatness is not in the amount of money you make, the position you hold, or the fame you achieve. It is in whether at the end of the journey, your hope pushed you beyond the expectations of others but within the capacity God gave.

We often hear people talk about "changing the world." You may think that's not a job that you're qualified to do. Think again. You may not personally bring peace to the Middle East, end hunger, or cure AIDS. But changing the world starts with changing *you*! It's about being willing to "grow where you're planted." You probably won't be asked to head up the Federal Reserve if you don't balance your own checkbook; you probably won't be asked to write a bestseller if you haven't even written a letter; you won't likely be asked to start as quarterback in the Super Bowl if you don't even exercise on a daily basis. Your chance to do big things depends on your willingness to do little things where you are, but if you are willing to take on the tasks that are before you and do them well, you will discover that your reward is not a sum of money but a much more challenging assignment.

Rather than think that your life experiences have kept you from achieving your full potential, see your life experiences as giving you the necessary tools and training *for* your full potential! Your hardships and even your failures are as much a part of your résumé as are your college degrees and your work experiences. The people I'd least like to be led by are those who have never known brokenness and have always had the best of the best. A person who has only known privilege has little understanding or patience with others. A person with some scars who has been to the bottom knows how to appreciate the top and what it means to be there.

Before your levees break and leave you stranded, take HOPE and head for HIGHER GROUND!